Computer Activities

for the Cooperative Classroom

Computer Activities

for the Cooperative Classroom

Linda M. Schwartz / Kathlene R. Willing

Pembroke Publishers Limited

© **2001 Pembroke Publishers**
538 Hood Road
Markham, Ontario, Canada L3R 3K9
www.pembrokepublishers.com

Distributed in the U.S. by Stenhouse Publishers
477 Congress Street
Portland, ME 04101
www.stenhouse.com

We acknowledge the financial support of the Government of Canada through the Book Publishing Industry Development Program (BPIDP) for our publishing activities.

Canadian Cataloguing in Publication Data

Schwartz, Linda M
    Computer activities for the cooperative classroom

Includes index.
ISBN 1-55138-129-X

1. Group work in education – Computer-assisted instruction. 2. Computers – Study and teaching (Elementary) – Activity programs. I. Willing, Kathlene, 1937–   . II. Title.

LB1028.5.S457 2001   372.13'60285   C00-932640-5

Editor:	Cynthia Young
Cover Design:	John Zehethofer
Typesetting:	JayTee Graphics

Printed and bound in Canada
9 8 7 6 5 4 3 2 1

For Cecil and Michiomi
— Linda and Kathlene

Acknowledgement

Throughout our journey of integrating computers into the curriculum, our students at United Synagogue Day School and The Bishop Strachan School have allowed us to grow as teachers. We have learned much from them.

It has been a privilege to share professional dialogue with the teachers who have participated in our workshops. They have raised thought-provoking questions about using computers with their students and have graciously exchanged ideas. Their dedication assures us that all teachers do have the skills to integrate computers into their curriculum.

The professional scope at both The Bishop Strachan School and United Synagogue Day School is appreciated. We pay tribute to the staff at both schools. They give us the opportunity to collaborate and they support our ideas. United Synagogue Day School provides the progressive environment critical to the development of computer integrated curriculum. Gilda Iron, Principal, Richmond Hill Campus, encourages creative computer initiatives. The Curriculum Council at The Bishop Strachan School has been an invaluable committee in which to learn about new assessment tools. Kim Gordon, Vice Principal, Curriculum is generous in sharing her ideas and materials. Susan Barter, Vice Principal, Junior School provides the freedom to develop the ideas. Many thanks to Catherine Dolan and her Grade Four students for the opportunity to collaborate on the Medieval unit.

We greatly appreciate the professional commentary of our pedagogical readers: Kim Gordon, Ziona Bordan, and Lori Rothschild. Their perceptiveness in reading the manuscript was most valuable.

Many thanks to our families for their enduring patience and encouragement. Michiomi A. Kabayama made constructive comments when reading the manuscript. He also made sure we did not skip lunch! Heartfelt thanks to Cecil Schwartz for his indulgence and for putting the project into perspective, often with humor, always with understanding and enthusiasm. Thanks also to Sara T. Schwartz, for her insightful reading of the manuscript, the circle is now complete; and to Devora and Ely Schwartz, whose support nourished their mother.

Table of Contents

Introduction: Implementing Change

The longest journey begins with but one step.

Chinese proverb

As a teacher, you have been expected to embrace and incorporate educational trends. Most likely, the creative and practical implementation of these new ideas has been left to your discretion. Today, you have the additional responsibility of integrating computers into your existing curriculum. Whether computers are located in your classroom, a lab, a resource centre, or in another area, using them as sound educational tools presents challenges that will be addressed in this book.

While striving for excellence, you may find yourself in a period of transition. Including technology in your teaching may prompt you to ask yourself some probing questions:

- Will my professionalism and teaching values be undermined by this technology?
- Will my personal teaching style be outmoded?
- Where will I find the time to add computers to my busy schedule?
- What do *I* do while my students are working with computers?
- How should I react if my students have more technical expertise than I do?
- How can my students benefit from using computers?

We have found that technology can be suitably adapted to support learning in several ways. Teachers who are already integrating computers have discovered that technology enhances their teaching. Their students use computers for diverse activities, such as writing and drawing, creating databases and spreadsheets, analyzing and organizing data, and communicating and researching on the Internet. Since these are important skills for the future, their early development is beneficial. These teachers also recognize the benefits of both linking their students with others around the world and using computers collaboratively within the classroom.

You Have the Expertise

Even though you probably have an appreciation of the educational value of computers, it may still be difficult to take the first step to actually start incorporating them into your program. You can confidently rely on your repertoire of successful teaching techniques as the foundation for computer

Be proactive! Actively seek out and work with colleagues who have developed computer-related materials and units. These colleagues are an integral part of the sharing and learning process.

initiatives. Given some practical suggestions, you can transfer and adapt your knowledge and strategies to include computers.

Teachers benefit from sharing a collective broad range of skills and experience. Many teachers, through developing computer curricula, teaching computer workshops for their colleagues, evaluating educational software, and attending conferences, have already become experts in the use of computers in their classrooms. By becoming experts, they are equipped to be professional mentors.

Our Vision

As Computer Resource Teachers in two different schools — one of us teaching at the Primary Level, and the other, from Kindergarten to Grade Eight — we share a common vision: Computer use should be seamless, transparent, and an integral part of all areas of the curriculum. Since students are enthusiastic computer users, this book will demonstrate how to direct their eagerness and guide them through the process of learning to use computers effectively.

With a clear focus on curriculum, we have developed practical computer activities based on the familiar cooperative learning model. The computer skills are learned incidentally to the content.

We would like to share our ideas with classroom teachers who are novice computer users, as well as with those who are more experienced, but who may not have had the time or opportunity to develop integrated computer activities. We assure you that this task is not as daunting as it may appear!

We recommend that administrators read this book and give their staff the time, training, and encouragement to implement the activities presented.

This book is primarily for teachers in the Elementary Division. However, many of the ideas in the book can be modified and appropriately used at Middle and Secondary Schools and Community Colleges.

Scope of the Book

Computer Activities for the Cooperative Classroom has a broad scope. Our goal is to present a complementary balance of content, process, literacy, and technology. The classroom-ready ideas presented in this book are intended to help the novice get started and to provide the expert with some fresh approaches for using computers in a social context.

An Overview of the Chapters

• **Chapter 1: Learning Cooperatively With Computers**

This chapter is devoted to the principles of cooperative learning. The focus is on communication skills, roles of group-members, social interaction skills, and ways to develop and introduce these into the learning environment.

Computers have been traditionally perceived as an individual activity. However, they can also be used effectively within the social framework of cooperative learning.

The activities included in this book, based on the methods and principles outlined in this first chapter, offer innovative collaborative learning opportunities, as well as some exercises for individual work.

• **Chapter 2: Assessment and Evaluation**

Assessment and evaluation are essential components in all teaching and learning. Chapter 2 provides samples of current assessment tools for cooperative learning using computers. We include formative and summative assessment tools for both teachers and students. These tools are Reproducible Masters that you may adapt to suit specific needs.

Valid assessment should not be limited to traditional methods. Accurate evaluation must be multi-faceted and include observations, the finished product, the process, student self-assessment, and their personal reflections.

Not all student work needs to be evaluated; however, the process should be continuously monitored. The process includes working cooperatively, comprehending, following directions, and effectively assisting peers. Involving students in peer- and self-assessment gives them ownership of their skill development and encourages them to define their goals and become committed stakeholders in the learning process.

- **Chapter 3: Developing Keyboarding Skills**

Keyboarding is a fundamental competency in using computers. We address the issue of keyboarding in Chapter 3 and provide a continuum of skill development.

- **Chapter 4: Integrated Activities**

Chapter 4 is comprised of three sections containing cooperative activities that incorporate the computer. The sections are organized by grade levels:

- Kindergarten to Grade Two
- Grades Three and Four
- Grades Five and Six

Computer skills are integrated into the content and presented developmentally to provide a wide scope. Some of the activities are intended for off-computer use. Our intention is to foster a varied and challenging learning environment. The activities refer to specific software, methodology, and grade level, and include suggestions to support students in learning subject content as well as computer skills.

The activities present a task that requires following instructions and making decisions. Both of these competencies develop comprehension and encourage HOTS — Higher Order Thinking Skills (Evaluation, Synthesis, and Analysis), process thinking, sequential thinking, and problem solving. The integrated activities offer students multiple opportunities to work cooperatively, yet become independent learners who develop a continuum of problem-solving strategies. We also recommend extensions for related activities and modifications to accommodate individual learning styles.

- **Chapter 5: Implementing a Cooperative Medieval Unit With Computers**

In Chapter 5, we look at how cooperative activities and computer use were implemented within the framework of a Grade Four Medieval Unit. The process that is outlined can be transferred to other units in other grades.

- **Chapter 6: Incorporating the Internet Into the Classroom**

This final chapter, written by an expert in the field, explains how to incorporate the Internet effectively. Although ethical issues with respect to the Internet are specifically addressed in this chapter, it is not within the scope of this book to discuss computer ethics in the broad sense. We have carefully developed the activities so they reflect and teach responsible, acceptable, and curricular-related Internet use. However, it is recommended that an *Acceptable Use Policy*, signed by both student and parent (or guardian), should be an integral part of a school's computer plan in order to ensure responsible computer use. For sample Acceptable Use Policies, search the Internet for "acceptable use policy."

Which Computer Platform?

Platform is irrelevant, as the activities can be generated in either a Mac or Windows environment, using any open-ended software tool. Where appropriate, we suggest specific software.

Taking the First Step

This book is intended to serve as an introduction and an impetus for teachers to use computers creatively. Computers by themselves do not offer improved learning opportunities for students, either as a class or individually. What makes the difference is the way in which the computer technology is used.

Use this book to initiate a "computer integration" journey. As noted earlier, the most difficult step in a new direction is often the first one. We hope the ideas and suggestions presented in the following chapters will encourage teachers to take that first step, and will make it interesting and professionally rewarding.

1 Learning Cooperatively With Computers

Computers are often perceived as solitary devices that isolate their users from other people and from social activities. This is a misconception. Computers can bring people together who might otherwise never have an opportunity to meet. They can enable people to work together in ways that were never thought possible.

Frank Smith

Synergy flows through the classroom when students work in small groups. Teachers know that group work provides students with opportunities to use both expressive and receptive modes of learning. Speaking and listening, representing and viewing, writing and reading, as well as thinking, can be maximized in group situations. Studies in group behavior point out that the quality of interaction in groups has an important influence on learning.

Where Do Computers Fit Into This Process?

Computers provide students with a natural place to gather for learning from one another. When students gather around a computer, they can exchange and discuss ideas in meaningful ways. Regardless of how students are grouped — by number, ability, interest, background, or gender — they share a common goal. Their task requires them to make decisions and, in most cases, to read. As they read and discuss, they interact dynamically and their thinking skills become apparent. They compare and contrast ideas, refer to the text, hypothesize and predict outcomes, reflect on and draw upon personal experiences, generalize and formulate conclusions, analyze, put new information into context, and make judgments. Furthermore, they usually stay on task.

When teachers observe students working together on a computer, the interactions of the students lead to valuable insights. The learning process becomes visible: students are observed using metacognitive strategies as they grapple with decision-making and their supportive behaviors are also in view. These observations allow teachers to implement diagnostic teaching tools. Conversations and actions reveal that members of more successful groups use and share a variety of communication roles that encourage cooperative learning.

What makes cooperation possible? Grouping students, in itself, does not necessarily ensure success. It is important to teach and model the skills overtly, as well as to understand the elements that comprise cooperative learning.

Elements of Cooperative Learning

These elements, as outlined by Johnson and Johnson (1990), incorporate the following five ideas. Every member must:

- share the goal;
- work in close proximity and have meaningful dialogue;
- be responsible for the successful outcome;
- use effective communication and social skills to ensure successful group work; and
- evaluate the group's collaborative efforts, as well as their own, and make adjustments when necessary.

With each individual focussing on the process of their own group, the teacher has a special role: to act as a facilitator for the small groups and to ensure that both the social and academic goals are processed in the class as a whole.

Why Are Some Groups More Successful Than Others?

Sometimes teachers attempt group work and find it disappointing. Communication is an important key to successful cooperative group work. Initially, students are not equally adept in using communication skills effectively. Some may not even have the social skills necessary for success. If students are expected to work effectively in groups, they must acquire the requisite tools to become skilled communicators and social beings.

Teaching and modeling the desired communication skills are essential and should be introduced in the course of regular classroom activities. When communication strategies are taught, students participate as cooperative group members. Students develop group communication skills naturally when teachers provide them with interesting tasks and opportunities for practice. Computers provide an opportunity for students to gather and communicate. In this environment, computer use also becomes a part of the learning. The skills that students learn from the overt teaching of cooperative skills can be applied to group work at the computer. Close proximity of students around a computer forces face-to-face interaction.

Part of the teaching and modeling process is to inform students that there are different ways of working and interacting — and that each way has its own purpose and value.

To foster group cooperation, model and teach appropriate communication habits, such as listening, courtesy, speaking up, and not dominating the conversation. You can also structure a supportive environment in which each student has a chance to observe, demonstrate, and evaluate group behavior. Meaningful group activities will create interest and help students to work together readily.

Three Ways to Work and Interact

Individual

- **I win or I lose.**
  There are times when it is necessary for us to work alone and our goal is personal. For example, doing something that is important to us alone, such as taking a test, drawing a picture or composing a story.

Competitive

- **If I win, you lose.**
  There are times when competition is appropriate. For example, in sports or contests the aim is to win.

Cooperative

- **If I win, you win.**
  Other times when we work together to reach a common goal, we must work as one. That is when cooperation is essential, such as working on a video production, a play, or a project that involves the computer.

Communication Skills

What skills facilitate cooperative learning? When adults work in small groups, they generally assume cooperative communication roles by asking questions, stroking egos, focusing on problems, and keeping discussions on track. Adult participants have the experience to take on different roles in the group dynamic without having the roles specifically assigned. For example, a participant may be a skeptic, or devil's advocate, to stimulate debate so that others can to clarify their ideas. If they are working in a successful group, the other members of the group are probably making similar contributions.

Labeling communication roles — skeptic, facilitator, clarifier, questioner, timekeeper, or reinforcer — makes the roles easier to understand — especially for children. Encourage your students to analyze the kinds of statements or phrases that help to identify each role. Although the roles are not mutually exclusive, presenting them separately will be helpful for students.

Identifying the Communication Roles

The following chart shows the kind of statements and questions that typify the roles and encourage active participation by all members of the group.

Role	Typical Statements/Questions	What They Do to Help
Facilitator	• What do you think, (name)? • You read this and I'll do that. • If we both read two lines, we can...	– directs the group to accomplish the goal – brings others into the discussion – helps with time management – delegates tasks so information is processed more effectively
Questioner	• I don't understand... • It doesn't make sense that... • What does (word/concept) mean? • How does that fit in? • If that's the case, then why...?	– questions are the first step in creative problem-solving – brings problems into focus – provide catalysts for clarification – questions/answers can help others who are more reticent – is a form of helping behavior
Skeptic (Devil's Advocate)	• What makes you so sure that...? • If we choose that, it won't work because... • That won't change anything. It will just... • Suppose that happens? Then what?	– provokes further discussion – a doubter who ask the uncomfortable questions – demands support/explanations – opens opportunities for others to think more profoundly or to offer appropriate rationale
Clarifier	• "Hoof it" means to walk. Like a horse — horse's "hooves"! Get it?	– gives explanations – is prompted by questions – helps others understand and solidify their thinking – offers more than just the "right answer"; answers lead to further explanation that stimulates and supports understanding
Reinforcer	• Thanks, (name). That helped. • Your explanation made it clearer for me. • I liked your idea about... • Let's use (name's) way. It sounds like it will work.	– supports others – makes general positive contributions (courtesy, praise, support) – focuses on ideas, not personalities
Timekeeper	• Let's take five minutes for this. • Each person has one minute to present. • We have fifteen more minutes. • Ten, nine, eight... • One, two, three...	– monitors amount of time left or used – helps to keep group focused, on task, and on time

It is essential for all students to become stakeholders in all aspects of the group process. Use one of the following two methods to enable students to become stakeholders. Using the first, more traditional method, the teacher arbitrarily assigns or allows students to select a role. The roles are rotated for the duration of the project within set parameters established by the teacher. (More mature students, with prior experience in cooperative learning, can be responsible for choosing their own roles.)

All roles are not necessary in every activity. Students may need to work through a few activities before they are comfortable with all the roles.

The ultimate goal of cooperative learning is for students to be able to transfer the roles into other situations.

Social Interaction Skills

Positive social interaction skills to consider:

be supportive
show kindness
listen actively
take turns
be polite
take responsibility
work out conflicts
be assertive
control anger
move quietly
be inclusive
use praise
use quiet voices
contribute ideas
ask questions
pace group work
negotiate differences
accept differences
celebrate success
follow directions
show respect
be considerate

In the second, more non-traditional method, all the students are responsible for learning each role. The teacher structures the process and provides a self-evaluation tool that encourages students to experiment with various roles as they work within their groups.

The teacher structures and guides the process in a cooperative learning activity. The teacher chooses a number of key roles, empowers all students to make spontaneous decisions, and provides evaluation tools. The students decide which role to play, learn when it is appropriate to switch roles, and assume the different roles cooperatively. Students also evaluate themselves in all the roles.

Assessment tools that are used when students are learning the cooperative process can be used as a reference point for reflection in subsequent projects. One such tool is the Individual/Group Self-Assessment. (A Reproducible Master for it is on page 18.)

Teaching Cooperative Learning Skills

Cooperative learning requires that students have an open mind so they can explore the dynamics that each group role encompasses. Students are expected to become adept in all roles and to gain the confidence and flexibility to shift roles when necessary. This reflects the authentic circumstances in which adults automatically assume roles depending on the situation. It also ensures that students are always engaged in the progress of their group, and this encourages inclusiveness.

As part of your classroom management strategies, incorporate the ongoing practice of these roles as they apply to all aspects of learning, including computers. Use brainstorming statements, or questions that exemplify the roles, as a springboard for role implementation. In small groups, students compile a list of defining statements and questions for the roles to present to the class. This type of communication exercise can be integrated in many other classroom activities.

T-charts and Y-charts

Developing and incorporating T-charts is a useful strategy to help students understand the purpose of communication and social interaction skills. A T-chart has two columns. Use the desired skill as the title and the headings *Looks Like* and *Sounds Like* for the two columns. Students brainstorm to describe actions and statements associated with the particular skill.

Students should also explore the emotional realm of communication and social interaction skills. Expand the T-chart into a Y-chart by adding a third column, *Feels Like*. In addition to what a skill looks like and sounds like, students brainstorm to identify how a particular skill feels emotionally. The Y-chart on page 19 shows descriptions that Grade Four students compiled when analyzing the skill of Active Listening. A Reproducible Master Y-chart appears on page 20.

Individual/Group Self-Assessment

Student Name _____

Social Skill	Myself	Group	Comments
FACILITATOR			
Staying on task			
Taking turns equally			
TIMEKEEPER			
Pacing group work			
Watching the time			
QUESTIONER			
Asking for help or clarification			
Asking useful questions			
Contributing ideas			
SUPPORTER			
Sharing materials			
Expressing support/praising			
Being courteous			
Being self-controlled			
Using quiet voices			
Including everyone			

Computer Activities for the Cooperative Classroom by Linda M. Schwartz and Kathlene R. Willing

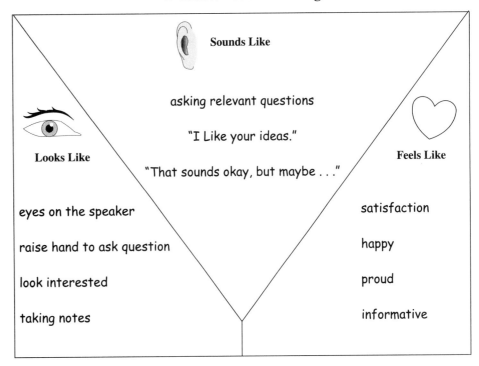

Y-Chart: Active Listening

Sounds Like

asking relevant questions

"I Like your ideas."

"That sounds okay, but maybe . . ."

Looks Like

Feels Like

eyes on the speaker

raise hand to ask question

look interested

taking notes

satisfaction

happy

proud

informative

Supportive Environment

It is important to create an environment in which learners feel supported in what they say and do. Learners definitely benefit from seeing, hearing, and feeling cooperative communication skills in action. That is why modeling is of the utmost importance. Many of the illustrative statements and questions associated with roles and skills can be used with students throughout the day.

To facilitate cooperative learning, a supportive classroom environment should be established at the beginning of the school year because students are more receptive to new ideas and expectations then. However, implementation at any time is always beneficial. The most important factor is to be comfortable with the approach. Making students feel valued and gaining their trust are essential.

To help students understand the underlying helping behaviors inherent in cooperative learning, encourage them to focus on and understand their own feelings. Help them become aware of how they react when positive and negative events occur. They can share their feelings with the class in various ways, such as drawing faces to show emotions or writing about personal experiences. When they have focused on how they feel or react, they can more readily appreciate how others feel. Students can also respond to open-ended statements, such as:

- "When someone hits me, I …";
- "When I do well in school, I …";
- "When I'm accused of something I didn't do, I…";
- "When I am happy, I …"; and
- "When I am mad, I …"

Y-Chart: _____

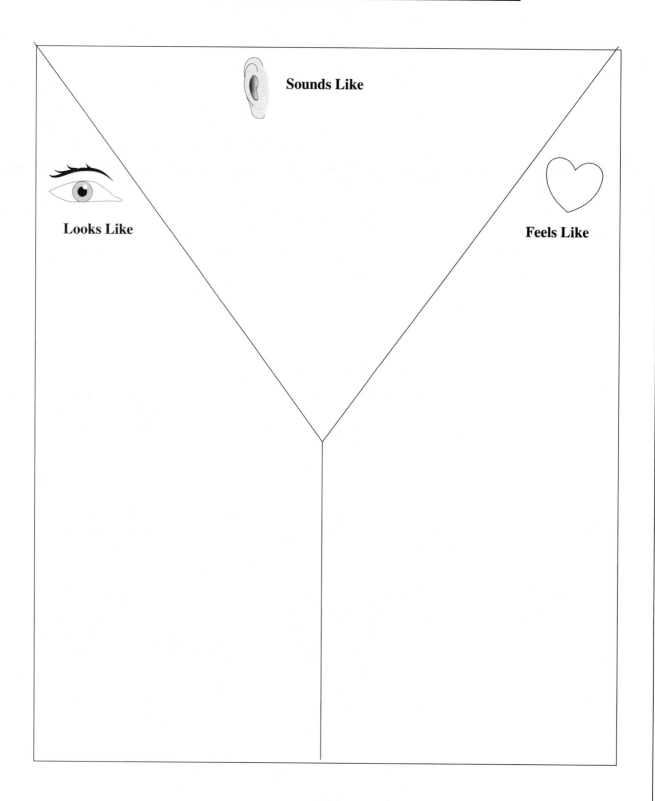

Sounds Like

Looks Like

Feels Like

Computer Activities for the Cooperative Classroom by Linda M. Schwartz and Kathlene R. Willing

Even very young students can learn to appreciate their own and others' feelings. Use a familiar idea with young students — traffic lights and the terminology associated with them.

- **Red light statements** stop us. They make us feel bad about ourselves and make others feel bad about themselves.
- **Green light statements** let us go. They make us feel good about ourselves and make others feel good about themselves.
- **Yellow light statements** are neutral. They do not affect us one way or the other.

Use the traffic light terms and statements to reinforce these concepts in other classroom activities. Younger students enjoy playing games. Using the traffic light concept, tell them that when you make a green light statement, they advance one giant step. They take one giant step backward for a red light statement, and they remain in the same spot for a yellow light statement. Encourage students to discuss the three kinds of statements and their feelings.

Other reinforcements include creating a web with a traffic light in the middle to categorize the statements and impromptu role-playing where students use the statements in pairs or small groups. Students can also brainstorm statements that can be listed on chart paper and then discussed by the whole class.

Conflict Management

Often students may not be aware that choices are available to them when conflicts arise. Even if they are aware, they may sometimes think in extremes. Discussing different ways of resolving issues helps students become aware of their power to make choices and successfully act upon them. They can be shown that strategies, such as *compromise*, *consensus*, *majority rule*, and *agree to disagree* are available to them when working with others and that all the strategies are equally valid.

- **Compromise** Each party gives up something in order to gain something. For example, "I could accept that if this were changed..."
- **Consensus** Everyone agrees.
- **Majority rule** A vote is taken to see which position is the strongest.
- **Disagreeing agreeably** When agreement can't be reached, then agree amicably that you cannot agree and move on to something else.

Model and explain the variations of conflict resolution so students can understand the ideas and see the differences. T-charts and Y-charts are also valuable for teaching conflict management. Have students brainstorm a T-chart for *Disagreeing Agreeably*. Their ideas should be similar to those in the sample chart on the next page.

Disagreeing Agreeably	
Looks Like	**Sounds Like**
Eye contact and handshake	I understand what you said, but you might want to think of…
Smile as you say something	I see your point, but have you thought about…
Members of the group listen to each other before saying anything	I don't agree because…
Shrug your shoulders	That's interesting, but…
Nod your head yes	If we do that, I think _____ will happen
Look up in the air as you agree	Okay, let's move on to something else

Role playing is another way for students to experiment with new ways of resolving conflicts. Allow them to role play both individual and group situations, looking at the scenarios from everyone's point of view. Students might role play situations such as the following:

- Your group is deciding on whose drawing will appear on the cover of your group report.
- An older student has just cut in front of you in line.
- A classmate has taken your pencil crayons without asking permission.
- Your class has only one soccer ball. Your group wants to use it at recess, but another group has gotten to it first.

Role-playing can be used in combination with a T-chart. Students observe another group role playing and then develop a T-chart that describes what was happening. Another strategy to help students resolve uncomfortable group decisions is to establish the criteria together with the students or create a rubric ahead of time. The criteria can then be used for the group evaluation that follows.

To heighten younger students' awareness of conflict resolution, develop a problem solving chart with them. Title the chart, "Settling Disagreements." The chart should include ideas such as those listed below.

Settling Disagreements
• Ask for help. A teacher or respected classmate who is not involved can give an objective opinion.
• Avoid the argument. Acknowledge disagreement and do something else.
• Compromise. Work out an arrangement incorporating each person's ideas.
• Postpone the debate. Wait until emotions have cooled.
• Share whatever it is. Work together.
• Take turns. One can do it now, the other later.
• Take a vote. Count opinions.
• Use humor. Make a joke of the situation to ease the tension so that constructive problem solving can occur.

The Computer and Cooperative Learning Groups

Computers bring students together. They offer an exciting forum to gather for a collective purpose. As students practice their communication skills at the computer, they learn cooperatively and develop technology skills in the process.

The kinds of cooperative tasks students are assigned when working at a computer should focus on decision-making and problem-solving to guide them in different ways of thinking; be open-ended and flexible so students can experiment with alternatives; and permit interaction for groups to discuss a common goal.

The teacher is the best judge when it comes to determining groups. Consider the following factors and answer these questions about students when you are planning group activities.

Forming Student Groups
• Personalities – How do they work together?
• Abilities – At what level are they working?
• Interests – What do they have in common?
• Opportunities – Who hasn't worked together?

Participating in groups is a broadening experience, which exposes students to others who are different. Students benefit from developing cooperative group skills with classmates who differ in gender, personality, ability, ethnic background, and interest. Encourage students' growth and insights by changing groups regularly to provide diversity and challenge.

2   Assessment and Evaluation

In short, we see authentic assessments — learning activities that closely resemble the ways that students will be expected to use their knowledge and skills in the real world.

Grant Wiggins,
Live and Learn, 1997

Assessment and evaluation of student progress are ongoing, demanding, and challenging responsibilities. However, they can be less onerous when thoughtful attention is given to the kinds of assessment and evaluation used for both process and product. A broad range of tools may be incorporated in assessing and evaluating all areas of the curriculum, including computers. Sample tools for both assessment and evaluation include:

- Rubrics
- Reflection
- Self-assessment
- Portfolios (both traditional and electronic)
- Student-led conferencing

Assessment of feelings, conflict resolution, and communication skills (oral and written) are best achieved by observing and listening to students. Authentic assessment is based on methods that reflect real-world situations such as cooperative teamwork. What students say and do and how they relate to their peers become important criteria. Therefore, both teachers and students need to develop their observation and listening skills. Such authentic assessment is particularly useful in judging criteria, such as observations of social interaction skills and group work, which are complex and subjective.

Rubrics

A rubric is a form of authentic assessment that measures performance. It is a scoring guide designed to appraise both individual and group activities that simulate real life. A rubric outlines the expectations or criteria and defines the levels of expected student performance. The expectations describe knowledge or a skill. The levels indicate the degree or frequency the knowledge or skill is employed by the student. A rubric offers many benefits to students and teachers.

The Benefits of Using A Rubric

A rubric
- allows for greater objectivity and ensures consistency
- clarifies the criteria in specific terms
- demonstrates clearly how students' work is evaluated
- promotes student awareness about criteria and its use in assessing peer- and self-performance
- can be used to measure performance throughout various stages to identify and monitor patterns and progress
- provides useful feedback regarding effectiveness of instruction
- provides benchmarks against which to measure and document progress

Levels in a Rubric

Level 1 – rarely exhibits the knowledge or skill

Level 2 – sometimes exhibits the knowledge or skill

Level 3 – usually exhibits the knowledge or skill

Level 4 – always exhibits the knowledge or skill

Cooperative Group Rubrics

When students are working individually, they reflect and assess themselves. However, when they work in cooperative groups, they must also include their peers in the assessment process. When students are familiar with the collaborative or cooperative learning process as outlined in Chapter 1, the next step is to develop a rubric.

A Cooperative Group Rubric assesses group activity and involves students in the developmental process. The rubric focuses on measuring stated objectives (performance, behavior, or quality); uses a range of levels to rate individual and group performance; identifies specific performance characteristics for each level; and is created in appropriate formats and levels of complexity for use by teachers and students.

As students become more familiar with rubrics, they will be able to participate in the process of constructing the rubric. This process empowers them, and their learning becomes more focused and self-directed.

To create a rubric, make a list of the expectations or criteria. Then, assign the levels and expand them with details that specifically address each of the criteria. The rubric for the activity, "Phun-Phonics" (Chapter 4, page 44), relied on observing the students and analyzing their products. Four expectations or criteria were developed.

- Fluency – alternating from stamp mode to writing mode
- Time on task – number of items completed within the time frame
- Originality – words and visuals demonstrate understanding of abstract concepts
- Phonetic awareness – using appropriate words to demonstrate the target sound

Rubrics become checklists! The criteria for the rubric can be predetermined by teachers, or evolve through class discussion and brainstorming. Both students and teachers may use the checklist. This process helps to make students responsible for their learning.

After these criteria were outlined, the details were added to create the rubric with four levels.

Phun-Phonics Rubric

Name _____   Date _____

	Level 4	Level 3	Level 2	Level 1	Level Score
Fluency	always is fluent in switching from stamp mode to writing mode	usually fluent in switching from stamp mode to writing mode	sometimes is fluent in switching from stamp mode to writing mode	rarely fluent in switching from stamp mode to writing mode	
Time on task	always has many images and words	usually has many images and words	sometimes has many images and words	rarely has many images and words	
Originality	always has many original ideas or abstract concept words	usually has many original ideas or abstract concept words	sometimes has many original ideas or abstract concept words	rarely has original ideas or abstract concept words	
Phonetic Awareness	always has appropriate words for target sound	usually has appropriate words for target sound	sometimes has appropriate words for target sound	rarely has appropriate words for target sound	

Comments: _____

_____

_____

Determining Criteria and Levels Using Webs

Ideas can be organized in a web to provide students with a visual summary of the discussion. Webs allow students to link new information with familiar concepts, summarize ideas, observe similarities and differences, draw conclusions, and consolidate information.

The links in the web will develop as the class discussion unfolds, and the criteria will become apparent during a brainstorming session. Once students are familiar with webbing, as modeled by the teacher, they can follow the example in their groups, or in pairs. In the following web, students in a Grade Four class brainstormed group expectations for cooperative learning.

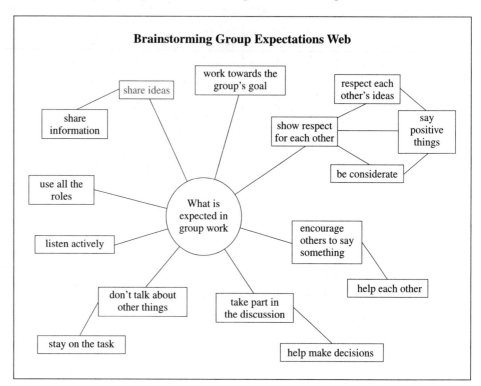

The criteria from the web can be sorted and developed into four expectations about the cooperative learning concepts and roles. (The students who developed these expectations were comfortable and familiar with the concepts and skills for cooperative group learning.) After the brainstorming, the class compiled their ideas about how they would collaborate. Their list included:

- work towards the group's goal
- share information and ideas
- make sure all the roles are being used
- show respect for others, be considerate
- participate in discussion and decision making
- encourage others to participate
- listen actively
- keep on task

Then the teacher established four distinct levels of achievement for the rubric the teacher and students would develop later.

- Level 4 – thorough understanding of the collaborative process

The Roving Reporter

Observation and listening skills are important for the teacher, too. The teacher plays the role of "roving reporter" to determine the students' progress in developing communication skills. Moving from one group to another, the teacher listens to students and observes their behavior. Exemplary comments that typify the communication roles, as well as areas for improvement, are brought to the students' attention. The focus is on what was said and how it worked. Encourage students to think about how the discussion advanced or was organized; how speakers responded to positive feedback; whether or not the feedback resulted in a new or improved idea; and how the skeptic in the group stimulated the discussion or affected the outcome.

Three Stars and a Wish

When young students are able to write on their own, you can use the "Three Stars and a Wish" technique. "Three stars" refer to three things in the activity that give students a sense of pride, and "the wish" refers to something they would like to improve.

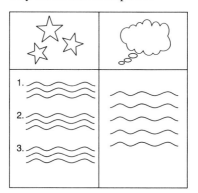

- Level 3 – good understanding of the collaborative process
- Level 2 – satisfactory understanding of the collaborative process
- Level 1 – does not yet understand the collaborative process

Students reworked the phrases to describe the cooperative learning process. In the final step, the teacher and students put the phrases in a matrix to form the Cooperative Group Rubric found on page 30.

Reflection

Reflection is essential to growth. All students are capable of some degree of reflection. This reflection can also be applied to their computer work. The younger they are when they start the reflective process, the more insightful it becomes as they advance through the grades. Setting specific criteria with students before starting a project is necessary. Portfolios and conferencing are useful tools that depend on reflection. Portfolios contain the material for reflection. Conferencing provides the venue for discussion. Younger students, who are not yet proficient writers, have the opportunity to answer simple questions that stimulate their reflection. Their answers help the teacher and/or the students set future goals. Asking questions or prompting students with open-ended statements can help them begin the reflective process. Expect deeper reflection from older students and ask them questions that demand more introspection.

Questions/Sentence Starters for Younger Students	Questions for Older Students
<ul><li>What did you make/do?</li><li>How did you make/do it?</li><li>What do you like about it?</li><li>What did you learn?</li><li>If you had to do it again, what would you change?</li><li>This work makes me proud because…</li><li>By doing this work, I learned…</li><li>This work was challenging for me because…</li><li>This work shows how I was able to …</li><li>Although this work was a challenge, I…</li></ul>	<ul><li>Why is this work included in my portfolio?</li><li>What makes this piece of work unique?</li><li>What process did I use to do this work?</li><li>What difficulties did I encounter?</li><li>How did I resolve the difficulties?</li><li>What was satisfying about the process?</li><li>What improvements will I incorporate into my next piece of work?</li><li>What did I learn in the process?</li></ul>

Self-Assessment

Students begin to assume responsibility for assessing themselves when they begin to reflect on their work and skills. A checklist can be used in any grade as a framework for developing questions about students' progress. This tool is especially useful when considering computer skills.

Students can assess their acquisition of computer skills with a self-assessment checklist, which should define a specific set of skills. Students are expected to master the skills by the end of the year. Levels of proficiency from dependence to independence are established. Students use the checklist for reflection and to check their progress at regular intervals. Teachers use it as a formative assessment to design and guide instruction.

Cooperative Group Rubric

Name _____   Date _____

	Level 4	Level 3	Level 2	Level 1	Level Score
Participation	always works towards the group's goal	often works towards the group's goal	works towards the group's goal with some asking	has to be reminded to work towards the group's goal	
Responsibility	voluntarily shares information and ideas	shares information and ideas without being asked	shares information and ideas with some asking	shares information only when asked	
Roles	always makes sure that all roles are used	makes sure all roles are used most of the time	occasionally makes sure all roles are used	rarely makes sure all roles are used	
Supportive behaviour	always says encouraging things to others	often says encouraging things to others	sometimes says encouraging things to others	needs reminding about others' feelings	
Active listening	always listens and responds	usually listens and responds	sometimes listens and responds	rarely listens and responds	
Goal oriented	actively keeps group on task	keeps group on task most of the time	sometimes keeps group on task	needs to be reminded to stay on task	

Comments:_____

_____

_____

Computer Activities for the Cooperative Classroom by Linda M. Schwartz and Kathlene R. Willing

Since students' computer skills progress along a continuum from Kindergarten to Grade Six, self-assessment checklists can be initiated or incorporated at any grade level. Modify the checklist for non-readers by using symbols to represent the tasks. Stamps or stickers can replace checkmarks. A sample checklist, The Computer Skills Assessment — Level 3 defines basic computer operations expected at a Grade Three level. (See page 32.)

By Grade Three students are expected to demonstrate proficiency in identifying the parts of a computer system, understanding terminology, keyboarding, and retrieving and saving files.

Each item in the checklist reflects the general skills that are emphasized throughout the year. Students reflect periodically about where they think they are in relation to each item and how much help they need. "No help" means they know how to do that particular skill without asking anyone and can help others if asked. "Some help" means they occasionally are not sure and sometimes ask classmates or the teacher to clarify or show them how to do it. "Lots of help" means they often need someone to guide them through the process. The checklist is completed with a written reflection on the back.

Portfolios

Select, reflect, and collect. These three verbs summarize the method and purpose for creating portfolios. Portfolios are collections of student work that represent a history of learning, growth, and change. They can include handwritten assignments, hard copies of computer work, electronic copies of computer work (digital photographs, disk or CD), art work, photographs, video tapes, and audio tapes. The portfolio provides meaningful documentation of effort, progress, and achievement, and it may follow students through several grades. Students are expected to understand the criteria for selection and judgment, participate in the selection of portfolio content, and include evidence of reflection for each entry.

Portfolios support strategies that emphasize the student's role in constructing understanding. They cover a diverse range of subjects, goals, and audiences for the student's assignments. As they select work for their portfolios, students should consider the following questions:

- What piece should be included in the portfolio?
- What would I like to re-read?
- What would I like to share with my parents or a friend?
- What makes this piece of work special to me?
- How does this piece of work show what I have learned?

The teacher works with the students to develop the criteria for selection depending upon the purpose of the portfolio. Is it to show *growth* or is it to showcase *best work?* Criteria for inclusion in a portfolio might include knowledge of the content, evidence of computer integration, knowledge of concepts, evidence of skills achieved, depth of reflection, quality of the product, cross-curricular connections, variety of entries, and organization and presentation.

Older students are better equipped to determine their selections independently after becoming familiar with the criteria. Younger students may need more direction in deciding which work their portfolio might contain. If the portfolio is

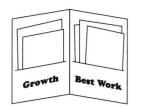

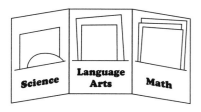

Portfolio Tip: Portfolios highlight different aspects of learning for a diverse array of subjects and skills. It is feasible and practical for students to have more than one portfolio or a single portfolio that is divided for several subjects/purposes.

Computer Skills Self-Assessment — Level 3

Student Name _____

Computer Operations			
I am able to do the following with:	**No help**	**Some help**	**Lots of help**
Turn the computer on and off			
Use the mouse to highlight and select			
Draw with the mouse			
Know the parts of the computer system			
Know the difference between a file and a folder			
Know how to log on using a password			
Know what "navigate" means			
Find my folder on the network			
Know the difference between "Save" and "Save As"			
Create a new document			
Name a new document			
Save a new document			
Rename a document			
Know where to save a new document			
Open an existing document			
Save an existing document			
Use both hands for keyboarding			
Use the proper fingering technique			
Use touch typing			
Open and close a folder			
Quit a program			
Be a good computer tutor			

Computer Activities for the Cooperative Classroom by Linda M. Schwartz and Kathlene R. Willing

to show growth, samples might include a variety of work completed in cooperative groups with explanations of the student's role and effort; the first, second, and final drafts of a piece of work; examples of best and worst work with an articulation of the differences between them; samples collected over time that show patterns; and similar work completed at different times of the year.

If the portfolio is showcasing a student's best work, it might contain an exemplary multi-media presentation; a social studies test with a high mark; a well-written science experiment; a superb solution to a difficult math problem, including all the rough work; a piece of creative writing showing editing for correct spelling and grammar; a reading-journal entry demonstrating depth of understanding of a character; and an outstanding piece of art work.

Use technology to provide variation in the way that students' work is presented. An electronic portfolio is a dynamic format that goes beyond paper and pencil. Students can display their work on the World Wide Web (www) or on a school Intranet for parents and friends to view. Knowing that others will see their work on the Internet is a powerful incentive and encourages students to be active learners — setting and reviewing goals and assuming responsibility for their learning.

The accessibility of an electronic portfolio makes it a concrete tool for discussion purposes. Parent conferencing takes on a new dimension because the electronic portfolio provides a more detailed and complete picture of the student's achievements. Writing, oral reading, art work, photos of three-dimensional models, animations, and presentations are easily collected in an electronic portfolio. The content evolves as students add new work. The electronic portfolio can be maintained and updated each year. Meaningful links between related work make cross-referencing possible.

Student-Led Conferencing

Student-led conferencing is a three-way dialogue between the student, the teacher, and the parent(s)/guardian(s). It is initiated by the teacher and led by the student for the purpose of reporting the student's progress to the parent(s)/guardian(s). Student-led conferencing actively involves students in the reporting process and provides a framework for them to become literate communicators, self-directed learners, and collaborative contributors to the reporting process.

Use the students' portfolios to help them review and revise their goals. In the conference, students show parents their work, talk about the units they studied, describe their favorite or best piece of work, explain incomplete assignments, and highlight their strengths. The conference provides a positive setting in which all three parties can explore strategies for improvement. Start preparing students as early as Kindergarten to conduct a student-led conference.

Early in the school year, instruct students about collecting their work in a portfolio and explain its purpose. During the conference, the reflection sheet that accompanies each item can serve as a script, which can calm an anxious student in some situations. A parent portfolio review and response sheet is included and can be modeled on the "Three Stars and a Wish" technique described on page 29.

Prior to the student-led conference, involve students in setting an agenda. A typical pattern for the conference is to:

• introduce the parent(s)/guardian(s) and teacher

- explain the purpose of the portfolio
- share portfolio contents
- explain what and why items are included
- invite parents' comments
- set goals
- thank parents for coming

Allow adequate time for students to rehearse with each other and compose an invitation to their parent(s)/guardian(s). The invitation is attached to a formal letter from the teacher that explains the conference.

While the conference is in progress, the teacher takes notes. These are subsequently used as a guide to formulate questions about setting goals and making decisions. A copy of the notes is filed in the portfolio for future reflection by the student. Later in the year, the student rereads the notes from the conference and writes a reflective paragraph outlining their progress. This goes into the portfolio and a copy is sent home.

Creating an Electronic Portfolio

Decide on the purpose. The purpose for collecting student work in an electronic portfolio should be clear. Is it for self-evaluation and goal setting? Is it to be used as a communication tool for learning? Or is it to be a snapshot of progress? Whatever the purpose, the electronic portfolio should not include everything a student produces. Therefore, identify the learning that is to be measured, and provide students with the necessary supporting activities that generate the material. For example, if "computer competency" is being assessed, the finished products should include samples of word processing, drawing, spreadsheet, database, and multi-media.

Select tools to assess the portfolio. Presumably, individual pieces of the student's work in the portfolio will have been assessed. However, it is also necessary to assess the portfolio as a whole. Appropriate assessment tools for an electronic portfolio are the same as for a traditional portfolio — measure the process students followed and their perception of their learning.

Select content of the electronic portfolio. The criteria for selection is a wide range of work samples that represent the student's progress. Electronic portfolios document the process of the learning task. Students should ask themselves:

- What do I plan to accomplish with this task?
- How do I plan to get there?
- What are my strategies for accomplishing the task?

Students may include interim evidence, such as notes on progress and summaries, of what made up the learning task. Draft versions, outlines, final products, and even unfinished products should be considered for inclusion. Discussion with the teacher may help students decide on the material, but ultimately students are responsible for the final selections based on the criteria. They review the electronic portfolio periodically and add new materials. Encourage peer review with an exchange of feedback!

Organize the electronic portfolio. Electronic portfolios should be organized to reflect an accurate picture of the student's development. Students should include a Table of Contents, a description of the task, a reflection for each entry, and any relevant links. Each piece of work should be dated.

3   Keyboarding Skills

They're just seeing the keyboard as a tool to get their ideas on the screen.

Georgina Hancock

A Basic Computer Literacy Skill

Keyboarding is a basic computer literacy skill, fundamental to all computer activities. Proficiency in keyboarding allows students to use the computer effectively as a tool for curricular integration without having to spend time hunting for the keys. Therefore, it is necessary to include keyboarding as an integral, ongoing component of the computer curriculum, beginning in Kindergarten.

Keyboarding can be viewed on a continuum from Kindergarten to Grade Six and can be divided into three broad levels.

Three Levels of Keyboarding	
Kindergarten–Grade Two	– keyboard awareness
Grade Three–Grade Four	– formal introduction to keyboarding
Grade Five–Grade Six	– independence in building speed and accuracy

Be a Computer Tutor

Encourage students to help each other using the "point and explain" method. This "hands-off" technique builds communication skills. Students must describe how to do something on the computer, but may not touch the keyboard. They may only point to the keys and explain what to do. They must not do the operation themselves!

Designate a computer area or learning centre in the classroom. A rotational schedule ensures that all students use the computer on a regular basis. Send students to the computer to do a specific task that relates to the curriculum — not as a reward! To develop independent computer users, post the schedule, general procedures, specific instructions, and some student computer work on an adjacent display board.

Make sure the student's name and the date is always on each piece of work. Keep the original for portfolios and display copies on bulletin boards. As students progress throughout the year, they can observe improvements in these displays. Displaying their work also shows that it is valued!

Keyboarding in Kindergarten

Kindergarten is a time for discovery. It is also the time to introduce keyboard awareness. Young students should become acquainted with the keyboard, the mouse, and the concept of using two hands. They also begin to understand the relationship between the mouse, the keyboard, and what happens on the screen. The first word they should learn to key in is their name. Teach them the

Figure 1
Grade One student sample of
keyboarding — journal entry

Figure 2
Grade One student sample of
keyboarding — letter to Degas

locations of the Shift Keys, Space Bar, Return/Enter, and Delete/Backspace. Then let them explore on their own.

Since the Primary years are when handwriting skills are emphasized, the amount of keyboarding expected from Kindergarten to Grade Two students should be minimal.

- **Discovery Stage** Allow Kindergarten students to explore the keyboard — discovering the location of letter and number keys. To get started, encourage them to type randomly. Print the first page only. They will soon start typing words they know. The length of this stage will vary, depending on the amount of time spent on the computer, a child's manual dexterity, and individual readiness.
- **Words Stage** The next stage is for students to type their name and any words they know — one word per line. This gives them practice using the Return Key. They may also key in words they see around the room. Print a copy and date it for them.
- **Sentences Stage** Incorporate the computer into a Language Experience activity. Brainstorm and record thematic sentences and display them on a chart near the computer. Students choose one sentence to key in and then illustrate the text. Using *Kid Pix Studio®Deluxe,* they can type the sentence as well as draw the picture. However, a word processing program can be used if a drawing program is not available. An illustration may be added later by hand.

Keyboarding in Grade One

Develop keyboard awareness skills in Grade One. This is an opportune time to systematically teach students where letters can be found. Reinforce use of the general purpose keys taught in Kindergarten, but add another component — a system to recall key locations with colors. Young students easily remember color-coded rows with names. For example, the "Blue Bird Row" is for number keys, the "Green Bunny Row" is for the top letter keys, the "Red Home Row" is for the middle letter keys, the "Brown Worm Row" is for the bottom letter keys, and the "Orange Spaceman" is for the Space Bar. This system emphasizes using two hands, learning the Home Row keys, learning that all vowels except "a" are in the "Green Bunny Row," and that the period and comma are in the "Worm Row."

It is important for students to learn the Home Row. The fingers always start on Home Row and return to Home Row when they begin to find the letters and numbers as they learn keyboarding skills. Simple phrases can provide metaphors to help students find the keys — "fly up to the Bird Row," "jump up to the Bunny Row," "crawl down to the Worm Row," or "thumbs for the Spaceman."

As students are learning the metaphor, provide tasks that reinforce keyboard awareness. At first, students can key in their own handwritten work, for example, entries from their journals. When students are ready, move to the next step, and have them compose brief paragraphs at the computer. Figure 1 and Figure 2 show examples of student keyboarding work.

Keyboarding in Grade Two

Reinforce the keyboard awareness skills introduced in Grade One by providing a wider range of keyboarding activities. Invite the children to type lists of words that have something in common. They might type lists of adjectives; verbs; nouns; things that move on wheels; animals; or places in the community.

Compose descriptive paragraphs based on social studies, math stories, science comparisons, and language arts book reports. If this activity is done in *Kid Pix Studio® Deluxe,* the text can be illustrated. Additional keyboarding ideas can be found in the Kindergarten to Grade Two Integrated Activities in Chapter 4.

Keyboarding in Grade Three

Our observation is that Grade Three students are motivated to learn formal keyboarding. Since eye-hand coordination and handwriting skills are sufficiently developed by Grade Three, it is the ideal time to introduce correct keyboarding technique before students develop bad habits. As the curriculum becomes more demanding, the expectation is that the presentation of content be more sophisticated. By Grade Three, students are beginning to have an awareness of the aesthetics of presentation. They realize that the appearance of their work is important and that keyboarding is essential to enhancing the presentation.

The rationale for teaching keyboarding to Grade Three students in a structured framework is that they are ready to learn touch-typing. They can learn as a class or independently. To maintain motivation and interest, use a balanced approach that combines teacher-directed learning with software-directed learning. Using the former approach, the teacher systematically guides the class through a series of steps to learn the keyboard and to practice. The latter approach relies on keyboarding software intended for independent, self-paced instruction. Self-directed programs such as *Mavis Beacon Teaches Typing!™*, *All the Right Type™*, *Type to Learn™*, and *UltraKey®* may also be used to supplement a comprehensive system and encourage independent skill-building. Once keyboarding and proper fingering are introduced, schedule regular practice sessions and provide integrated activities to help students maintain the skills. (See Chapter 4 for ideas for appropriate activities.)

Teaching keyboarding is challenging! It is time consuming and requires careful preparation and scheduling. The ongoing challenge is that it demands constant reinforcement. *Typin's Cool™* is a system that organizes and simplifies the task. It provides a comprehensive package that includes all of the necessary materials and a unique method for learning the location of the keys. Scheduling suggestions, a sample implementation plan, video tapes, practice sheets, text books, progress charts, and software make the task less daunting for teachers. Support for *Typin's Cool™* is easily accessible. (See the Appendix.)

Keyboarding Tip: Although we recommend that *Typin's Cool™* be introduced in Grade Three, the system is versatile and can be implemented in any grade.

Keyboarding in Grade Four

In Grade Four, students build on the skills learned in Grade Three. Start the school year by showing the *Typin's Cool™* video to reinforce the proper fingering technique. Introduce this program to students who have not used it

Most Important at This Level:
Provide students with adequate
practice time and a variety of
activities!

before. If you have other students who used the program in Grade Three but did not complete the *Typin's Cool*™ textbook or all the practice exercises, they may continue from where they left off.

At the computer workstation, provide a CD of classical music and a set of headphones. The first part of this activity is to listen to the music and at the same time key in single adjectives or point form phrases that describe the music. Students save and print one copy. In part two of the activity, they use the printout as jot notes for composing and typing a short essay. Prompt students with these open-ended statements:

- The music makes me feel…
- The music makes me think of the color…
- I associate this music with…weather.
- I associate this music with…
- I would name this piece of music…

Link keyboarding to curriculum! Students can practice keyboarding by composing character and setting descriptions or plot summaries at the computer. You might have students key in a poem that they have written on a social studies theme. See the Grade Three and Grade Four Integrated Activities in Chapter 4 for more keyboarding ideas.

Multi-task — Students can combine their keyboarding skills with their use of the Internet! Instruct students to log on to an art site and select a piece of art to describe. The artwork is left on the screen while they open a new word processing document. After arranging both windows side-by-side, they key in their description as they view the art. You can prompt students with open-ended statements similar to those for the descriptions of classical music.

Keyboarding in Grades Five and Six

Assuming that formal keyboarding has been introduced in an earlier grade, Grade Five and Six students will be ready to develop speed and accuracy independently. Start the school year by reinforcing proper fingering technique. (Present the *Typin's Cool*™ method if students have not yet been introduced to it.) Make supplemental programs available so students can practice on their own. Encourage further independence by posting a weekly schedule so that students can sign up for practice sessions. At the beginning of the year, inform students that some assignments will be designated as "keyboarding exercises." Explain that these exercises will be typed at school and that adequate class time will be provided. Also indicate that their grade will be the average of two marks, one for content and one for keyboarding and formatting. Refer to Chapter 4, Grade Three and Grade Four Integrated Activities for more keyboarding ideas.

4   Integrated Activities

The teacher is the most important and expensive piece of technology in the classroom.

Howard Pitler,
Principal, L'Ouverture Computer Technology
Magnet School, Witchita, Kansas

About the Integrated Activities

The integrated activities in this chapter use the curriculum as the vehicle to teach computer skills. These necessary skills are acquired incidental to the curriculum. Using our integrated approach, the technology is transparent and is seamlessly connected to the content. The activities in this chapter are divided into three sections:

- Kindergarten to Grade Two
- Grades Three and Four
- Grades Five and Six

We have developed practical computer activities based on the familiar model of cooperative learning. These activities follow a continuum of skill development from Kindergarten through Grade Six, and progress from the introduction of a skill, to the development of that skill, and to the extension of that skill in other applications. This continuum of skill development creates a standard for computer integration.

However, new technologies and variations in students' level of expertise will necessitate changes. To ensure progress along this continuum, some skills are repeated in different contexts.

Every activity in this chapter includes:

- Curricular Connections – how the activity integrates with the curriculum
- Computer Connections – the development of computer skills on the continuum
- Software – the recommended software
- Overview – an overview of general information
- Cooperative Connection – an opportunity for cooperative learning
- What to Do – instructions for implementation and templates
- Modifications – changes to accommodate individual needs

Some activities also include:

- Extensions – ideas to expand the activity
- Internet Ideas –Internet use is recommended where appropriate

Important Tip: We recommend that teachers read all grade-level activities to help them meet the needs of individual students. The framework for implementing the standard for computer integration may not yet exist in some schools. However, most activities presented in this chapter can be modified to suit other grades. For example, skills or concepts in an activity designated as Grade Two may be introduced to older students.

Choose any activity to start. Order the activities to suit your purpose. Each integrated activity is unique. Use the activities "as is," or modify them to spark your own creative initiatives.

About the Software

Use flexible software. We have chosen to use open-ended tool software, such as *AppleWorks*® and *Kid Pix Studio™ Deluxe*. We have intentionally avoided using content-specific software. It tends to be restrictive and does not allow for the same level of creativity. All recommended software is available on both Mac and Windows platforms.

Software changes. It is not uncommon for software to be updated, become obsolete, or for software companies to merge. These changes require flexibility. However, best practices, objectives of the activities, and the principles of cooperative learning remain constant for whatever software is used.

You can substitute software. Although specific software titles have been recommended for each activity, similar applications may be substituted. For example, where *AppleWorks*® is recommended, any tool software, such as *Microsoft*® *Works*®, *Microsoft*® *Word*®, *Microsoft*® *Excel*®, *Microsoft*® *Access*®, *Adobe Illustrator*®, *Adobe Pagemaker*®, is appropriate. Where *Kid Pix Studio™Deluxe* is suggested, any open-ended drawing or painting application may be used. Modifications in the What to Do section of a given activity may be necessary when substituting software.

Software Versions Vary! Many of our instructions are based on *Kid Pix Studio™ Deluxe* and *ClarisWorks* version 5.0.1 (now called *AppleWorks*® and is available for Windows), therefore some minor adjustments to the instructions may be necessary for your specific computer setup.

Integrated Activities — Kindergarten to Grade Two

Bunny Hops

Overview

Challenge students to a game of estimating and comparing. "Bunny Hops" develops computer skills as students learn about rabbit movement and habitat. They create a document in landscape orientation and draw a path that goes from a tree in one corner to a rabbit's burrow in another corner. How many hops will the rabbit take from the tree to the burrow? Students begin by typing their estimate at the top of the screen. Now it's time to check their answers!

Students use the *Kid Pix Studio™ Deluxe* "Rubber Stamps" to place rabbits on the path to compare their estimate with the actual number. When the game is finished, a descriptive sentence is typed at the bottom of the screen. Be prepared for enthusiastic and spontaneous discussion as students compare their results. Students enjoy describing the "Bunny Hops" process in a student-led conference.

Cooperative Connection

Blend a computer activity with seat work. Place students into cooperative groups of four. Have the group work at the computer to design a new path and corresponding estimate. Away from the computer, students write individual estimates on a four-column spreadsheet or chart with Name, Estimate, Reason

Curricular Connections

Math/ Language Arts/ Science
• estimating and measuring
• comparing
• following instructions in sequence
• descriptive writing
• identifying animal habitat
• describing animal movements

Computer Connections

• dragging out a perfect circle
• selecting thickness of pencil tool
• selecting a graphic object
• duplicating objects
• selecting and using typewriter tool

Software

• *Kid Pix Studio™ Deluxe*
• any Paint application
• CD ROM clip art

for Estimate, and Actual Number as column headings. They discuss which estimate is closest and then return to the computer to complete the activity. Back at their desks they complete the spreadsheet with the actual results. They evaluate both the group process and their individual efforts, which brings closure to the activity.

What to Do

- Discuss the process of the task, as described above. When students know what to do, give them a step-by-step demonstration using the following instructions.

    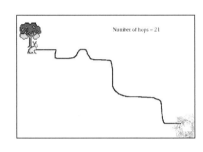

    1. Open a new *Kid Pix Studio™ Deluxe* document.
    2. Use the Circle tool to draw a burrow in bottom right corner.
    3. Select green from the Color Palette and use the Pencil tool to draw green grass around the burrow.
    4. Use the Rubber Stamp tool to add a tree in upper left corner.
    5. Select the Pencil tool, change the thickness, and draw a path from the tree to the burrow.
    6. Use the Rubber Stamp tool to stamp one rabbit at the beginning of the path beside the tree.
    7. Use the Typewriter tool to type: "Estimate = # hops."
    8. Use the Rubber Stamp tool to stamp enough rabbits to fill the path.
    9. Use the Typewriter tool to type a sentence that includes the actual number of rabbits on the path.
    10. Type your name
    11. Print in Landscape orientation.

Modification

- Depending on the subject or theme of the unit, any animal may be substituted for the rabbits, and the scenery can be changed to match the animal (e.g., penguins going from the water to the ice).

Extensions

- Ask the students to compose a paragraph or math story about the rabbits in a separate word processing document.
- Students could open a new document in *Kid Pix Studio™ Deluxe* and create a different path. They should compare the two.
- Once students know how to create the picture and use the tools, take the opportunity to engage students in a creative thinking activity at another time. Ask students, "What would happen if...
    - the rabbit's burrow and the tree were both on the right side of the screen and the rabbit had to go around a dog house on the left side of the screen?
    - the path was straight?
    - the tree and the burrow are both at the bottom of the screen and the rabbit had to climb a hill?
    - the burrow is in the middle of the screen and the rabbit had to go around two trees, one on the left side and the other on the right?"

Community Mural

Curricular Connections

Social Studies/ Math/ Language Arts
- categorizing and comparing
- counting
- graphing
- descriptive writing
- communicating information visually and orally
- identifying community helpers, buildings, and physical features

Computer Connections

- selecting and using rubber stamp tool
- selecting and using drawing tools
- editing in a graphic environment
- selecting and using typewriter tool
- opening, using, and renaming a template

Software

- *Kid Pix Studio™ Deluxe*
- any Paint application
- CD ROM Clipart

Overview

This is a two-tiered team activity. Students begin "Community Mural" by working individually to create a computer drawing based on the theme of community. They experiment with the *Kid Pix Studio™ Deluxe* "Rubber Stamps" — stamping the required components: houses, buildings, parks, playgrounds, zoos, and vehicles. Remind the students, "Don't forget the people!" When students complete their community drawing, they add a descriptive sentence. As always, students type their name and print the page.

The document is based on a "Road Template" created by the teacher. This template ensures that the road is evenly matched from one end of the mural to the other when each child's work is pasted together. The teacher develops a rubric with students that describes various levels of understanding of what comprises their community. Students may consider their individual contribution to the "Community Mural" as part of their portfolios.

Next, students work on the second tier of the activity to cooperatively assemble and paste the documents together.

Cooperative Connection

This activity combines computers and curriculum with cooperative team work. The teacher determines the size of the group and which students will work together. Each group completes the following phases.

- Group discussion – Before working on computer, the group briefly discusses details of each member's contribution to the community landscape.
- Individual tasks – Each member of the group creates several sections of the mural. (For each new section, students must access the "Road Template" again.) They will need to print each section.
- Group discussion – The group reassembles to determine the order in which the mural will be put together and how they will present it as a group to the class.
- Group task – The group pastes the mural together and presents it to the class.
- Group reflection – The group evaluates itself.

What to Do

- The first step is to create a "Road Template" before introducing "Community Mural" to students.

  1. Open a *Kid Pix Studio™ Deluxe* Document.
  2. Select the Rectangle tool.
  3. Select gray from the Color Palette.
  4. Drag out a gray rectangle from the extreme left to the extreme right of the screen. This rectangle, which represents the road, should be placed about a quarter of the way up from the bottom of the screen to leave room for a sentence or two.
  5. Select the Straight-line tool.
  6. Select yellow from the Color Palette.
  7. While holding down the Shift Key, drag out a straight horizontal line in the middle of the rectangle from left to right. This line divides the road.
  8. Select the Eraser tool.

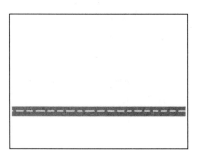

9. Click at evenly-spaced sections along the yellow line to make the dotted line.
10. Select the same gray from the Color Palette as selected for the road.
11. Select the Paint Bucket tool and fill in the white squares.
12. Save the document. Name it "Road Template."
13. Make the template available to students.

- Next, give students a step-by-step demonstration using the following instructions:

1. Open the "Road Template."
2. Use Rubber Stamp tool to select houses, vehicles, trees, community helpers, etc.
3. Create a sample Community landscape.
4. Demonstrate various methods of editing in a graphic environment: Undo function, different colors and sizes of Eraser tool, white paint in the Bucket tool, white Circle tool and Rectangle tool to cover mistakes.
5. Compose a descriptive sentence below the road. Type name.
6. Go to File menu and choose Save a Picture. Rename the document.
7. Print in Landscape orientation.

Modifications

- Modify the expectations based on the ability of the students. Sentences may be simpler or more complex. If time permits, some students may be expected to compose a descriptive paragraph.
- Encourage originality. Instead of using stamps, students can create original graphics by experimenting with combinations of the drawing tools and the Wacky Brush tool.
- Have students do some math activities after the mural is assembled and displayed. You might want to try the following ideas.
  - Sort and count various objects, such as vehicles, buildings, community helpers. Record the findings on a chart, then use them to create a graph.
  - Measure and compare the length of the community road using standard and non-standard units of measure.

Extensions

- Divide the class in half and create two different murals. Using the same format, have one half of the class create a mural of the urban community while the other half creates a rural community. Have the class compare the two murals by means of a chart and/or Venn diagrams. These activities may be done on or off computer. (See "Who Am I" for the Venn diagram template instructions, page 45.)

Internet Idea

- Telecollaboration is long-distance collaborative work. By connecting with other students from far-away places, your class can compare communities in other parts of the world. Log on to the Internet. Register with ePals. Use this Web site to search for a classroom with which to exchange community information. Participate in ongoing interactive projects. Individual students may also communicate with their peers around the world. http://www.epals.com

Phun-Phonics

Overview

Make phonics exciting with "Phun-Phonics." Students select the *Kid Pix Studio™ Deluxe* "Rubber Stamps" and type words to match a target sound.

Students type their name in a corner and the target sound in the centre. Next, they select the Rubber Stamp tool and search the rubber stamp database for an image to match the sound. They stamp the image on the screen, then use the Typewriter tool to type the word that matches the image. Give them a time limit for their first run with this activity. Use the average number of images and words students found within the time limit to create a rubric with your students. Repeat "Phun-Phonics" a few times and assess the students' results against the rubric.

When students are confident in the requisite computer skills, "Phun-Phonics" can be used as an independent or paired activity that encourages self-esteem through decision-making. Students may want to include several versions of "Phun-Phonics" in their portfolios to show their progress.

Cooperative Connection

Foster student ownership. Include students in the assessment process by working together to create a rubric that details the expectations.

This activity is an ideal opportunity to allow the students the independence to choose their own partner. Each pair then creates a document with a different target sound and they present it to the class. Based on the rubric, the groups evaluate their own work and process.

What to Do

- Give students a step-by-step demonstration, using these instructions:

    1. Open a new *Kid Pix Studio™ Deluxe* document
    2. Use Typewriter tool to type your name in the corner and the target sound (e.g. short "a") in the centre.
    3. Select Rubber Stamp tool and search for an image that has the target sound. Stamp the image on the screen.
    4. Select Typewriter tool and type the word next to the image.
    5. Repeat steps 3 and 4 for more images and words.
    6. Go to Goodies menu and choose "Pick a Stamp Set."
    7. Select a different Stamp Set and select OK.
    8. Repeat steps 3 and 4 again for more images and words.
    9. Print in Landscape orientation.

Modification

- Repeat "Phun-Phonics" throughout the year. Modify the activity to reflect the relevant consonant or vowel sound. Use beginning, medial, or ending sounds. "Phun-Phonics" encourages creative thinking by giving students the opportunity to make connections between abstract concepts and concrete images.

Extensions

- "Phun-Phonics" is multi-purpose. Let students use the concept to create a document relating to a target theme. In place of a sound, students type the

Curricular Connections

Language Arts
- phonemic awareness
- matching
- following instructions in sequence
- flexibility in thinking
- researching

Computer Connections

- selecting graphic objects
- using menu bar to switch rubber stamp sets
- typing words to match objects
- switching between two tools
- searching a graphics database

Software

- *Kid Pix Studio™ Deluxe*

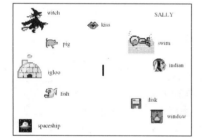

theme (e.g., structures, movement, or farm animals) in the centre of the screen. They search for and select appropriate images and type in the matching words.

- Challenge budding writers with abstract concepts, such as happiness. Encourage sentence building in addition to the individual words.

Who Am I?

Overview

Think of the possibilities! What happens when primary students compare themselves to an insect or a reptile? "Who Am I?" offers that opportunity. At the same time, students begin learning the skill of multi-tasking. They create a small self-portrait in *Kid Pix Studio™ Deluxe,* select an animal Rubber Stamp, and copy both into a "Venn Diagram Template." Next, they drag out text boxes and list the characteristics of each species inside the Venn diagram's circles.

If your application does not support drawing overlapping circles for a Venn diagram, use a one-by-three table and have students type three separate paragraphs. "Who Am I?" may also be completed entirely in *Kid Pix Studio™ Deluxe* without the multi-tasking component. Encourage students to present "Who Am I?" at a student-led conference.

Cooperative Connection

Since listening skills are essential to cooperative learning, include a game of "Say and Switch!" (Kagan 1990). In this cooperative structure, pairs of students take turns sharing information from their Venn Diagrams and listening to each other. The first partner shares with the second. When a signal sounds they switch — the second shares with the first. When the switch occurs, the students' challenge is to pick up from where the other partner left off. Allocate time so that several switches take place. Each student reports back to the entire class on something they learned from their partner. "Say and Switch" provides a cooperative framework in which to review concepts and check for understanding.

What to Do

- Create a Venn diagram template before introducing "Who Am I?" to students.

  1. Open an *AppleWorks®* Draw document.
  2. Go to the File menu and choose Page Setup. Select Landscape orientation.
  3. Reduce the screen view to 50% so that you can see the entire document.
  4. Select the Circle tool.
  5. Holding down the Shift Key, drag out a perfect 13-centimetre (5-inch circle). Make the circle transparent in order to see the overlapping lines.
  6. Select and Duplicate the circle.
  7. Place the circles side-by-side. Overlap the circles leaving adequate room for a text box in each section of the Venn diagram.
  8. Select both circles. Go to the Arrange menu and choose Lock.
  9. Save the template. Name it "Venn Diagram Template."

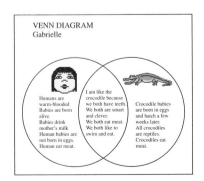

- To assist students with multi-tasking, give them a copy of the instructions on page 46. Review the instructions with the class and do a step-by-step demonstration. (We have observed that Primary students delight in being active participants in the demonstration. Their participation reinforces the instructions and assists in the transfer of ownership for following directions. They proudly read each step aloud and walk the class through the process.)
- Since this activity requires two or three sessions, the activity is presented in two parts. In part one, students create the *Kid Pix Studio™ Deluxe* document and multi-task by pasting the images into the *AppleWorks®* document. In part two, students compose and type the text.

Modification

- Encourage sentence building. Give young authors the opportunity to compose a descriptive paragraph using the vocabulary from their Venn diagrams. Compose the paragraph in a separate (word processing) document.

Extensions

- Build students' self-esteem. Primary students gain computer confidence by repeating multi-tasking activities. Substitute the content and reuse the "Venn Diagram Template" with other units that require sorting, comparing, and contrasting.
- Stimulate inquiry. Compile a class spreadsheet on or off the computer that summarizes all the animals students have researched. Use column headings, such as animal, number of legs, habitat, food, and species.
- Bring light-hearted closure to "Who Am I?" with a brain teaser activity. Print the Venn diagrams without the two images and the students' names. Randomly distribute the documents and challenge the students to play a guessing game off computer of "Who Am I?" Students deduce who it is and write the name of the person and the animal.

Writing Adventures

Curricular Connections

Language Arts
- organizing ideas in logical sequence
- communicating ideas
- revising and editing
- using correct conventions
- enhancing writing with other media
- building descriptive vocabulary

Computer Connections

- keyboarding
- using editing functions
- incorporating graphics
- formatting a document
- designing a page layout

Software

- *Kid Pix Studio™ Deluxe*
- *Amazing Writing Machine®*

Overview

In "Writing Adventures," students have an opportunity to develop writing skills. "Writing Adventures" is comprised of three activities. Depending on your time and students' needs, choose just one activity, or try them all. "Draw and Describe," "My Feelings Book," and "The Plot Thickens." All three produce excellent additions to Portfolios — electronic or traditional.

1. Draw and Describe

Overview

Foster active listening. Use "Draw and Describe" to build reading and writing skills. *Kid Pix Studio™ Deluxe* is an ideal application that inspires emergent author/illustrators. Young students use drawing tools to create a picture on a specific theme or topic. They use the typewriter tool to compose a description. "Draw and Describe" allows Kindergarten students, in particular, to take a first step in the writing process using the computer. Less is more — briefly describe

Who Am I? — Instructions for Students

Part One

1. Open a new *Kid Pix Studio™ Deluxe* document.
2. Use the drawing tools to draw a small self-portrait.
3. Choose an animal Rubber Stamp and place it next to your portrait.
4. Go to the Moving Van tool and choose the Lasso tool.
5. Use the Lasso tool to draw a circle around both images.
6. Go to the Edit menu and choose Copy.
7. Go to File menu and choose Save a Picture. Rename the document.
8. Now you are ready to leave *Kid Pix Studio™ Deluxe.* (Do not Quit.)
9. Open the "Venn Diagram Template."
10. Go to the Edit menu and choose Paste.
11. Choose the Arrow tool. Place the images above the Venn diagram. Resize if necessary.
12. Go to the File menu and choose Save As. Rename the document.
13. Go to File menu and choose Quit.
14. *Kid Pix Studio™ Deluxe* is still open. Go to the File menu and choose Quit.

Part Two

1. Open your *renamed* Venn diagram document.
2. Use the Text tool to drag out a text box.
3. Type words to describe yourself and move the Text box into the left side of the Venn diagram. Resize if necessary.
4. Use the Text tool to drag out a second Text box.
5. Type words to describe your animal and move the Text box into the right side of the Venn diagram. Resize if necessary.
6. Use the Text tool to drag out a third text box.
7. Type words to describe how you and your animal are the same. Place this Text box in the centre of the Venn diagram. Resize if necessary.
8. Use the Text tool to drag out a fourth Text box. Type your name and place it in the top right corner of the screen.
9. Go to the File menu and choose Save. Print a copy.

Computer Activities for the Cooperative Classroom by Linda M. Schwartz and Kathlene R. Willing

Clocks have numerals and hands.

Ophelie

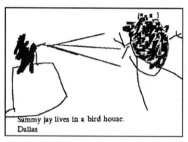

Sammy jay lives in a bird house.

Dallas

Tip: Integrate the visual/spatial. Put a simple drawing on the board to help students understand the concept of page layout. Start by drawing a line two thirds down from the top of the page. Explain that this line divides the screen — the upper part is for drawing and the bottom part is where they will write. Remind students to hold down the Shift Key when using the Line tool in order to draw a perfectly straight line across the screen. This can also be demonstrated on the computer.

the topic and activity then let them go to the computers. You will be astounded by the caliber of creativity that results from encouraging students to be active listeners during the introduction. Be adventurous…try the activity the other way. Describe and then draw!

Cooperative Connection

In "Draw and Describe," students draw, share, write, and share again, using the computer. In the final sharing, students present their pictures and descriptions to the rest of the class.

What to Do

- Discuss the value of sharing ideas. Use children's picture books to show how an illustrator and author work together. Usually they start with the words, and then the illustrator draws the pictures.
- Explain that in this activity, students start with the pictures and then supply the words.
- Choose a theme or topic. Then invite the students to draw a picture at the computer on the specified theme or topic.
- Students take turns working at the computer. One student completes their drawing, and types "Illustrated by…" on the work. The student exchanges places at the computer with another student, who composes a description of the drawing. When they are finished, they type, "Written by…"
- Print one copy for each student. When all the students have drawn a picture and written a description, the author and illustrator present their work together to the class.

Modifications

- Modify expectations with respect to the extent of details. This will depend on two critical factors: the varying levels of student ability and the degree of risk students are willing to take. "I can't draw!" is a familiar refrain. Respond with, "Of course you can! Here is how." Then guide the student's hand. Depending on manual dexterity, expect various levels of detail. Challenge students to write a detailed paragraph including descriptive sentences. Encourage reluctant writers by indicating that simple phrases are also acceptable.

Extensions

- Make it interactive! Students can read each other's work and exchange places at the computer a second time to peer edit.
- Compile finished work into a book for the classroom library. Laminate the cover page. These classroom treasures make excellent thematic resources.
- Incorporate it with a language experience. Use the vocabulary generated from a language experience activity. Place the language experience chart by the computer for easy visibility. Instruct students to choose and type a sentence or word from the chart. They illustrate their sentence or word. Print a copy for display.

Integrated Activities — Kindergarten to Grade Two

2. My Feelings Book

Overview

This activity fosters emotional awareness and its multi-page product complements an "All About Me" unit. After class discussion about a particular emotion, students use a series of color-coded templates to write about and illustrate their feelings. Depending on which emotions are discussed, choose headings, such as *In the Pink, Feeling Blue, Red with Rage, Scared Yellow,* and *Green with Envy.* The phrase, together with an appropriate graphic, combine to make each template. The project extends over several classes. Using a different template for each class, every student composes a sentence to match every template heading.

Tip: Go easy on your nerves, print each set of documents when students are not around.

Cooperative Connection

Use the cooperative structure of "corners" (Kagan 1990) to heighten students' awareness of emotions before sending students to the computers to start "My Feelings Book." This activity encourages introspection and allows students to analyze their own emotions. Make four posters, each one illustrating a familiar emotion, such as anger, sadness, happiness, or jealousy. Display each poster in one corner of the classroom.

The teacher poses questions and the students respond by going to the appropriate poster. For example, the teacher asks, "How did you feel when …?" When all of the students have selected a poster/corner, they pair up and discuss their reasons for choosing that emotion. After the discussion, one pair from each corner shares their reasons with the class. Students gain respect for each others' feelings when they listen to and share their diverse perspectives.

What to Do

- Create a template before introducing "My Feelings Book" to students. The page layout is the same one-third text, two-thirds visual/spatial formula used in "Draw and Describe."

  1. Open a *Kid Pix Studio™ Deluxe* document.
  2. Use the Typewriter tool to type the heading at the top of the screen.
  3. Add an appropriate graphic on either side of the heading. Use Rubber Stamps, import clip art, or scan pictures.
  4. Go to the File menu and Save a Picture. Name the document "Happy Template."
  5. Repeat Steps 1–4 saving each template with the name of a different emotion.

- Explain to students that they will work at the computer to describe and illustrate their emotions. They will access different templates for different emotions. They will write a sentence related to each emotion and then create a simple black line drawing for each one. Each sentence should begin with an appropriate starter, such as "I feel happy when…," "I was sad when…," "I get angry when…," "I am afraid of…," or "I was jealous of…" Each student also creates an illustrated cover page, personalizing it with the title, "(Student Name's) Feelings."

- Next, do a step-by-step demonstration for students, using the following instructions.
  1. Open the "Happy Template."
  2. Select and use the Typewriter tool to compose a sentence in the bottom third of the screen.
  3. Select and use the drawing tools to illustrate the sentence. Draw the picture between the template heading and the sentence.
  4. Select and use the Typewriter tool to type your name wherever there is available space.
  5. Go to the File menu. Choose Save a Picture. Rename the document "Happy *your name*."
  6. Quit *Kid Pix Studio™ Deluxe*.

- When all the pages are printed, compile them into books. Since parents appreciate being informed about students' work on computer, make the last page of the book a letter to the parents explaining the curricular and computer connections. (See the example below.) A little PR goes a long way! Consider making this a standard practice whenever you are sending computer projects home.

Dear Parents,

Your child has produced this booklet in the Computer Lab.

The project was designed to complement the

Grade One unit on Emotions.

This integrated activity has given the children the

opportunity to continue to develop their computer

skills within the context of their curriculum.

Linda Schwartz

Modification

- Some students will complete the "My Feelings Book" more quickly than others. Challenge those students to think of other emotions and design the appropriate pages. Emotions, such as peaceful, relaxed, or embarrassed can get the student started.

Extension

- Make it bilingual. The content of "My Feelings Book" is a familiar and universal theme. Create "My Feelings Book" using any two languages. It is not unusual for students to come to school speaking a language other than English. Students feel more comfortable writing about personal feelings in their native language first. The next step is to express the same emotions in their new language.

Tip: "My Feelings Book" may be created in any language!

Integrated Activities — Kindergarten to Grade Two

Tip: For those not familiar with *The Amazing Writing Machine*®, open the application and select Story and then select Write.

3. The Plot Thickens

Overview

Do you have access to only one computer? Use the cooperative structure, "Roundtable," (Kagan 1990) and the *Amazing Writing Machine*® or any word processing application to compose a cooperative story. The subject can be open-ended or based on a specific unit.

Cooperative Connection

Cooperative connections run throughout this activity. Students must share the computer cooperatively. To create the best story, they need to read, acknowledge, and incorporate the work of the previous writers. They share the story as a whole class at the end, and every student can take pride in having contributed to this unique composition.

What to Do

- Begin with a classroom discussion about the concepts of basic story structure — beginning, middle, and end. Explain that in this activity they will take turns adding sentences to write one story by several authors.
- Remind students that sentences always begin with capital letters and end with punctuation. Advise them that elements such as intrigue, humor, dialogue, and surprise should advance the logical progression of the story line. Since comprehension is integral to "The Plot Thickens," emphasize that best results occur when the next student carefully reads the previous writers' work before composing any additional sentences.
- Start the exercise by typing an opening sentence, then have students take turns working at the computer individually to add one or two more sentences. (Writers may identify their contribution by typing their initials in brackets before their sentences or by changing the color of the font.)
- Illustrations enhance the text. If possible, allow students to add appropriate visuals to the story.
- The final result is a unique story! Print out in small books or in large format.

Modifications

- For younger students, a continuous rhebus story (images replace some words) is easily created in *Kid Pix Studio*™ *Deluxe* using a combination of Rubber Stamps and the Typewriter tool. See the multi-tasking instructions, page 47. Demonstrate how to use the Moving Van tool and the Lasso option to copy and paste previously used Rubber Stamps.

Extensions

- Use story puzzles to reinforce comprehension and sequencing as an off-computer activity. Take the story produced in "The Plot Thickens" and double space and format the page so that each sentence appears on a separate line. Print multiple copies of the story. Cut each copy into individual sentence strips. Place each set of strips in its own container. Students work cooperatively in teams to reassemble the story.
- Older students can use *Kid Pix Studio*™ *Deluxe* to create mazes based on the events in the completed story from "The Plot Thickens." Students construct mazes using four concentric boxes created with the Box tool. They use the

Eraser tool to make openings and the Straight Line tool to make barriers. Suggest they test the maze with a thin line using a different colored Pencil tool. If the maze works, they erase the test line. To make this activity challenging, set criteria such as mazes must represent the beginning, middle, and ending of the story, and must include a minimum of three sequentially placed graphics. Every maze is printed, and students exchange them with each other or share them with a younger class for an off computer activity. When sharing with a younger class, older students read the story aloud with students first. Everyone enjoys this "a-mazing" experience!

Internet Idea

• Include telecollaboration to add an electronic dimension to "The Plot Thickens." Log on to the Internet. Register with ePals: http://www.epals.com. Use this Web site to find other classes to advance the story. This extension will likely take some coordination between you and the other teacher to ensure that students can access the computers in order to exchange and complete the story within a specific period of time.

Integrated Activities — Grades Three and Four

Animal Cubes

Curricular Connections

Math/ Language Arts/ Science
• measuring
• making Nets and constructing cubes
• researching animal facts
• factual writing
• editing

Computer Connections

• formatting a multi-page document
• selecting different fonts, sizes, styles and colors
• using spell checker
• selecting clip art from CD ROM
• downloading a graphic from Internet
• keyboarding

Software/Internet

• any word processing application
• CD ROM of commercial clip art
• CD ROM encyclopedia(s)
• online encyclopedia(s) (*World Book, Britannica*)

Overview

Challenge aspiring graphic designers with "Animal Cubes," an activity in which students use an innovative presentation for research. Students are guided through the process of synthesizing information from each of the following three sources: traditional library resources, CD ROMS, and the Internet to create an "Animal Cube."

The students choose an animal and prepare a six-page document about the animal: Students complete five topics for research: food, physical description, habitat, reproduction, interesting facts, and an illustrated title page.

Completed "Animal Cubes" are intended to be hung from the ceiling. Remind young graphic designers that this unique method of display demands exceptional layout and design. Their viewers should be able to read it comfortably and avoid a stiff neck! Encourage students to include the hard copy of "Animal Cubes" in their portfolios.

Cooperative Connection

If you have limited access to computers, and limited space for hanging up the finished Animal Cubes, grouping students into pairs or triads makes this a cooperative activity. As a team, they problem solve how to equitably assign individual research and writing. Rough drafts are read together and peer edited. Back at the computer, cooperative delegation of tasks occurs. Each team member is responsible for typing two or three pages. Spell checking (peer editing), cutting and gluing the pages onto the cubes are all cooperative efforts. Team evaluation brings closure to the project.

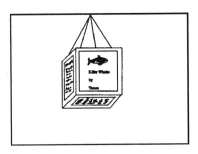

What to Do

- The first step is to create a 20.3-centimeter (8-inch) cube constructed of poster board. Students then measure the cube to determine the required document format. After completing the calculations, they make the necessary adjustments to the margins on the computer. They should incorporate a variety of fonts, sizes, styles, and colors in order to heighten the visual impact.
- When all the pages are finished, students spell check their document. Peer proofreading is the next stage in the editing process.

Formatting a Document

Give students a step-by-step demonstration, using these instructions:

1. Open a new word processing document.
2. Adjust margins according to the calculations.
3. Align to the Center for the title.
4. Select and change Font, Size, Style, and Color for the heading.
5. Type the title, Food.
6. Press Enter or Return twice and start typing the body of the text.
7. Realign text for left justification.
8. Select and change Font, Size, Style, and choose black for the color of the text.
9. Type the text.
10. To get to the next page, go to the Format menu and choose Insert Page Break.
11. Repeat Steps 3 to 8 for the remaining four research topics.
12. Move to the next page and make the title page.
13. Align to the Centre.
14. Select and change Font, Size, Style, and Color.
15. Type the name of your animal. This is your title.
16. Press Enter or Return twice and type your name.
17. Press Enter or Return twice and type the date.
18. Add a graphic image to the title page.
19. Spell Check the document.
20. Save and name the document, "Student Name Animal Cube."

Spell Checking a Document

Tip: *Edit, edit, edit!* The writer should always spell check the final copy before printing, and check the printed page(s) for general appearance and elements before handing it in for assessment.

Editing involves more than reading over the document. The editing process is done in stages. Begin the editing process by using the Spell Check function. Spell checking is an opportunity for students to reread their work; however, there are some things that teachers and students should know before using a computer's spell checker. Most often, it checks for spellings it knows or recognizes; but, some spell checkers *may not* identify errors such as incorrect spacing or punctuation, repeated words, homonyms, and correctly spelled words used in the wrong context. As well, the computer has a limited vocabulary database that does not include many proper names.

Students also need to understand that the computer does not correct the spelling for them, but only highlights words that it does not recognize. Some spell checkers provide options for the correct replacement. This allows students to be decision-makers when the computer highlights a word. With the *AppleWorks*® spell checker, the student can choose to Replace or to Skip.

Modification

- Students may have a broad range of writing skills. Expect variations in sentence structure, detail, and length.

Extensions

- "Animal Cubes" may be adapted for projects in other curricular areas. Novels? Construct a cube that highlights five events, five unique traits of a specific character, or five different characters. The sixth side is the title page. Countries, states, or provinces? Describe five areas of interest. Make the sixth side a map. Planets? Divide class into groups to investigate one planet each. Five sides describe aspects of the planet. Download an Internet image for the sixth side.
- Are some of your students inquisitive mathematicians? Let them research polygons and then create Nets (two dimensional layouts of polygons). They write a description of the polygon and format it so the text is presented in the shape of the polygon.
- Invite students to create an Animal Slide Show. (See the instructions for How to Make an *AppleWorks®* Slide Show.) Use the Slide Show function of *Kid Pix Studio™Deluxe* or *AppleWorks®* to present a visual summary of important facts in "Animal Cubes." Multi-tasking is necessary when building a side show. Open the "Animal Cubes" document, then open a new *AppleWorks®* Draw document. Edit the text to fit the screen. Change Font sizes and add more graphics. In Slide Options select Loop, which presents each slide show in a continuous loop.

How to Make an AppleWorks® Slide Show

You can create a slide show from any existing *Appleworks®* document (except communications) with multiple pages. Or you can create a new document with multiple pages. Each page in the document is one slide.

The best choice is a draw document because it is the most versatile. A master page with a common background design can be made. Frames, which act like windows in another layer, can then be used to combine different types of information, such as charts, text, spreadsheet data, and paint images in the same document.

1. Open or create the document from which you want to run the slide show.
2. Go to Window menu and select Page View.
3. Select the number of pages depending on the type of document:
   - Word processing – do nothing
   - Draw – go to Format menu and select Document. Enter pages across and pages down.
   - Paint – go to Format menu and select Document. Enter pixels across and pixels down.
   - Spreadsheet – go to Format menu and select Document. Enter columns across and rows down.
4. If creating a new Draw document enter the desired information and visuals for each page (slide). Check the Help function for further details.
5. Use the tools to add text, spreadsheets, charts, and other visuals.
6. Scroll through the document to check the slides.

To Run a Slide Show

1. Open the document you wish to view.
2. Go to the Window menu and select Slide Show.
3. Select the desired Options.
4. Press Start.
5. If the slide show does not advance automatically, click the mouse button to advance the slides.
6. Press "q" on the keyboard to quit the Slide Show.

Internet Ideas

- Give students who have time an Internet challenge. Ask them to download Internet images for each side of their cube.
- Students can check out the World Wildlife Foundation Web site. Have them log on to the Internet and collect information about animals and ecology at this comprehensive site. You and your class may want to get involved in online environmental and endangered species projects. http://www.wwf.org

Word Links

Curricular Connections

All Content Subject Areas
- reviewing vocabulary
- defining vocabulary
- spelling
- following instructions in sequence
- communicating information in a different format

Computer Connections

- selecting and grouping objects
- keyboarding and editing in a graphic environment
- selecting and using text tool
- selecting, locking, and unlocking objects
- using Shortcuts to duplicate objects
- designing a page layout

Software

AppleWorks®

Tip: Use key commands. By Grades Three and Four, students have learned how to copy and paste using drop down menus in the Menu bar. They are now ready to duplicate objects using the key commands method. Either the Command key or the Control key is used in combination with an alphabetic key. Check the drop down menus for the applicable key combination.

Overview

Use "Word Links" to help students reinforce vocabulary and develop page layout skills. Students brainstorm a list of subject-specific vocabulary and definitions, then select eight words that have a letter in common. Students work in pairs to create a simple crossword puzzle.

Cooperative Connection

In this activity, pairs of children work as a team to create a crossword puzzle. They both make word-lists, and must decide which words to use and which ones are vertical/horizontal. At the computer, they solve the following problems. How does the team equitably share the tasks? Who works at the computer? Who dictates the text? When do they switch? How do they know they were successful? The process concludes with group and self-evaluation.

What to Do

- Brainstorm a list of words related to a specific subject or topic. Organize students in pairs. Both students select and define eight words. Independently, they print each word horizontally on graph paper — one letter per square — and then cut out each word.
- As a team, they arrange and connect the words on standard letter size paper to form the word link. The team must decide which words need to be rewritten vertically. When all the words have been positioned, they paste them onto the paper. This draft version of the puzzle should also include the definitions.
- Once the teacher has checked the draft, students open a Draw document and use it to create the puzzle on the computer. Definitions are typed into two separate text boxes, one for the Down Clues and one for the Across Clues. Students may rearrange the puzzle and the clues to create an appealing page layout. Consider including a copy in the portfolio.

Inuit Puzzle
Kelly

Across ➡

1. Inuit winter home
2. Inuit summer home
4. Inuit used to eat mainly _____
5. Inuit transportation
6. Inuit used to be called _____

Down ↓

1. Eskimo is another name for _____
3. lamp to heat igloo
4. soap _____ carving
7. Eskimo means "eaters of raw _____

Inuit Puzzle
Kelly

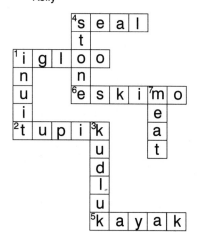

Creating a Word Link

- Because the instructions are detailed, the steps are divided into three sections: Creating the Word Link Squares on Computer, Adding Numbers to the Squares, and Adding the Title and Clues. Provide students with a hard copy of the following instructions and give a step-by-step demonstration.

Creating the Word Link Squares on Computer

1. Open a Draw document in *AppleWorks*® and reduce the view to 50%.
2. Use the Rectangle tool to drag out one square. Hold down the Shift key while dragging to get a perfect square.
3. Select the square, go to the Menu bar, and change the Object Size. The approximate size of the square should be 1.5 centimeters (five-eighths of an inch).
4. Select that square and Duplicate it. Use the rough draft to determine the total number of squares.
5. Using the Arrow tool, drag the squares into place. Use the rough draft as a guide.
6. Go to the Edit menu and choose Select All.
7. Go to the Arrange menu and choose Group. The squares can now be moved as one object (puzzle).
8. Position the puzzle. Leave room for the definitions.
9. Go to the Arrange menu and choose Lock. The puzzle cannot be moved. If it needs to be moved later, go to the Arrange menu and choose Unlock.
10. Return to 100% view.
11. Save.

Adding Numbers to the Squares

1. Number the puzzle squares. To do this, drag out a small text box anywhere on the screen.
2. Type "1" and move it into the appropriate puzzle square.
3. Duplicate the "1" text box. Change it to "2."
4. Move the "2" into the appropriate puzzle square.
5. Repeat the numbering process until all numbers are in position.
6. Go to the Edit menu and choose Select All.
7. Go to the Arrange menu and choose Group.
8. Go to the Arrange menu and choose Lock.
9. Save.

Adding the Title and Clues

1. Drag out a text box and type your name.
2. Drag out a second text box and type the title of the puzzle.
3. Drag out a third text box and type "Across." Press the Return or Enter key twice and type the definitions beginning each one with the matching number.
4. Drag out a fourth text box and type "Down." Press the Return or Enter key twice and type the definitions beginning each one with the matching number.
5. Arrange the puzzle and all text boxes: title, name, and clues.
6. Save.

Integrated Activities — Grades Three and Four

Modifications

- Increase or decrease the number of words students use in "Word Link." If the number of words is increased, add another challenge. Create an answer page by printing a blank copy and writing in the answers. Or, the answers could be added on the computer — drag out and position text boxes which contain the individual letters for each word. Save the original. Select Save As and rename the document "Word Link Answers." This keeps the original document intact and creates a separate document with the answers.
- Students may want to enhance the appearance of "Word Link" by adding graphics.
- Use "Word Links" to create a comfort level for students who would benefit from doing this activity in their native language.

Extensions

- *Parlez-vous français? Habla usted español? Sprechen sie Deutsche?* Use "Word Links" to reinforce vocabulary in another language.
- Compile a book of "Word Links" for use in the classroom.
- Use "Word Links" vocabulary to spark creative writing and poetry.

What Was It Like Then?

Curricular Connections

Social Studies/ Language Arts
- identifying characteristics and lifestyles of early settlers
- identifying geographical areas of early settlement
- researching and communicating information
- chronological sequencing
- writing from another perspective
- interviewing

Computer Connections

- formatting a multi-page document
- keyboarding
- selecting and using straight line tool
- grouping and locking objects
- adding clip art

Software/Internet

- *AppleWorks®*
- *Timeliner®*
- *Kid Pix Studio™ Deluxe*
- CD ROM clip art
- downloaded images from Internet

Make it multi-media! Use the digital camera to take pictures of their characters for display or slide show presentation. Video tape the production and use it as a self-assessment tool and a team assessment tool.

Overview

Children are fascinated with the lives and times of earlier societies. In this activity, students use the computer to create two timelines. The first is based on information (about the student), which they collect by interviewing one of their parents. For the second timeline, students create a fictitious person based on research and historical fiction about pioneer life or colonial times. Each timeline shows ten significant events and includes text and graphics. When both timelines are completed, the students compare the ten significant events and draw conclusions.

Cooperative Connection

Make this activity cooperative. Place students in teams of four to six to collaborate on all aspects of a one-act play. In preparation for playwriting, teach a lesson on writing dialogue using proper punctuation. As a team, students read their pioneer/colonial timelines and discuss how to connect the different characters into one play. Then they write a script on or off computer. Adding simple props, they present in costume.

What to Do

- Give students copies of the Reproducible Master "My Timeline" on page 60 for interviewing their parents. Explain that they will use the information to create a personal, illustrated timeline stretching from their birth to the present.
- Provide students with fiction and non-fiction resources about pioneer life and colonial times. When the students have finished their research, ask them to create an imaginary pioneer or colonial child. Using the "My Timeline" reproducible, they identify ten significant events and generate an illustrated, personal timeline for their fictitious person. The two timelines are displayed

Tip: As an alternative to the open-ended tool software referred to in the "What to Do" section, use a task-specific application. Students can create timelines using *Timeliner®*, which organizes data chronologically, includes graphics and text, and automatically formats the printing of the timeline banner.

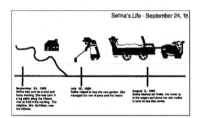

Tip: If the text is hidden behind the bubble, go the Arrange menu and choose either Move to Front or Move to Back.

together. Ask the students to compare, contrast, draw conclusions. Suggest that the timelines be considered for portfolios!

• Because the instructions are detailed, the steps are divided into three sections: Formatting the Timeline, Creating the Text, and Adding the Graphics and Title. Give students a hard copy of these instructions and do a step-by-step demonstration.

Modifications

• Encourage students to add speech bubbles or thought bubbles to the timeline. Go to File menu, select Library, and choose Balloons. Create text boxes for short comments or exclamatory statements. Place the text boxes inside the bubbles. Resize or flip the bubbles if necessary. When each bubble and text box is in place, select them both and go to the Arrange menu and choose Group.

• Students may opt to include more than the minimum ten events.

• Invite students to create timelines for different periods in history (e.g., Medieval or Roman Times).

• Students can scan and manipulate a photograph. For the students' own timelines, they import a scanned photograph of themselves into an *AppleWorks®* Paint document. They use the Eraser tool to remove the background of the picture, leaving only the face. Now they use the Pencil tool to add a costumed body and the appropriate hat. When the drawing is complete, they should Resize it if necessary, and use the Lasso tool to select the "new person." The last step is to Copy and Paste it into the timeline.

Extensions

• Create an *AppleWorks®* spreadsheet for comparative analysis of the two timelines. Have the students compare Food, Clothing, Housing, Education, Occupations, and Family Size.

• In preparation for the interviews, ask the students to brainstorm questions for the data sheet, role play the interviews, and practice note-taking skills during role playing to record information.

• In language arts, students can transfer information from the Pioneer Life/Colonial Times timeline into a journal format.

• Use the timeline format for any topic where sequencing is relevant. For example, students could delineate events in a novel or create a storyboard.

• Create a timeline in another language.

Internet Idea: ThinkQuest

• Celebrate life in colonial times on the Internet. Discover how people lived in the 1700s. This ThinkQuest was designed by Grade Four and Five students in Pennsylvania.
http://library.thinkquest.org/j002611F/

• Challenge students to become Web page developers and create engaging ThinkQuests for their peers. Visit the ThinkQuest Web site to discover how to participate.
http://www.thinkquest.org

Timeline

Formatting the Timeline

1. Open a new *AppleWorks®* Draw document
2. Reduce the view to 25%.
3. Go to File menu and choose Page Setup. Select Landscape orientation.
4. Go to Format menu and choose Document. In the Size window, type "3" in the Pages Across box.
5. Go to Window menu and choose Page View.
6. Select the Straight Line tool with 6 pt thickness. While holding down the Shift key, drag the line across all three pages.
7. Place the line about one-third of the way up from the bottom. Go to Arrange menu and Lock it.
8. Select the Straight Line tool with 6 pt thickness. While holding down the Shift key, drag out one short, vertical line, approximately one centimeter (one-half inch).
9. Duplicate the short line nine times. These will be placed along the horizontal line.
10. Go to File menu and choose Save.
11. Name the document "Student Name Timeline."
12. Save.

Creating the Text

1. Drag out a text box and enter the first event.
2. Repeat this process for the remaining nine events.
3. Place the text boxes below the horizontal line.
4. Place the short vertical lines on the horizontal line so that they touch the text boxes.
5. When the layout is complete, go to the Edit menu and choose Select All.
6. Go to Arrange menu and Lock.
7. Save.

Adding Graphics and Title

1. Drag out a text box and type the title. Place the text box at the top and centre of the timeline.
2. Drag out a second text box for your name. Centre the text box below the title.
3. Use graphics from different sources.
4. Create and import graphics from *Kid Pix Studio™ Deluxe*.
5. Go to File menu and choose Library.
6. Use downloaded clip art from the Internet.
7. Use CD ROM clip art.
8. Import scanned family photographs.
9. Place the graphics along the timeline.
10. Save.
11. Print and assemble the three pages into a timeline banner.

Computer Activities for the Cooperative Classroom by Linda M. Schwartz and Kathlene R. Willing

My Timeline

Student Name _____

Year	Important Event

Computer Activities for the Cooperative Classroom by Linda M. Schwartz and Kathlene R. Willing

North, South, East, or West?

Tip: As an alternative to the open-ended tool software referred to in the What to Do section, use the application, *Neighborhood MapMachine™*. It has all the necessary tools for drawing maps, includes pioneer graphics, and automatically formats the printing of the map.

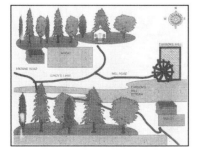

Overview

In "North, South, East, or West?" students explore the pioneer/colonial village. The activity allows students to demonstrate their understanding of mapping skills. Students conduct research about the major components of a pioneer or colonial settlement. They develop a rationale for the location of the settlement and the components within it. Next the students create their own layout of a settlement and generate it on the computer.

"North, South, East, or West?" can stand on its own or be combined with an activity such as "What Was It Like Then?" on page 57. Together, these activities make a fully integrated unit when students study their heritage.

Cooperative Connection

Invite your students to become town planners. Adapt "North, South, East, or West?" to involve the entire class in producing one large, detailed map. Using a variation of the cooperative structure, jigsaw, (Kagan 1990), group students to create sections of the map which represent specific areas of the settlement, such as shops, mills, farms, homes and school. Each group appoints a "Town Planner" who meets with the other Town Planners. They design the Master Plan of the settlement off computer. They then divide the plan by the number of groups.

Using the computer, each group drafts their assigned section to a uniform scale. Print the maps on heavy paper, glue on to poster board, or laminate because they will be combined to form the base of the settlement. Each group uses Lego to build the appropriate structures and then places them on the map. Use any adhesive or double-sided tape to keep the structures in place. Apply the same team dynamics as described in Chapter 5, page 82. Display and present in costume on Parents' Night!

What to Do

- Gather and provide resources about pioneer and colonial settlements. Explain that students will research and take notes on the major components of pioneer or colonial settlements. Ask students to compose a rationale for the location of the settlement and the individual areas that comprise it.
- Review mapping skills with the class. Then invite students to map out their research findings on computer. Give students a hard copy of the "Creating the Maps" instructions below. Do a step-by-step demonstration at the computer. Students' maps should include a compass rose, key, scale, labels, natural, and artificial landforms. Graphics of pioneer/colonial buildings can be added.
- Since students take pride in the "professional" appearance of their maps, you may want to laminate them. Assemble and display all maps with the written explanations. Suggest that students include the map in their portfolio. You could also compile the maps with the written explanations into a "Big Book" format with a suitably weathered-looking cover.

Creating the Maps

1. Open an *AppleWorks®* Draw document.
2. Go to the File menu and choose Page Setup. Select Landscape orientation.

3. Go to the Window menu and choose Page View.
4. Go to the Format menu and choose Document. Type in "2" Pages Across, and "2" Pages Down.
5. Reduce the screen view to 25% so that you can see the entire document.
6. Draw roads using the Pencil tool. Use 8 pt thickness. To make the roads connect with other settlement sections, begin and end all roads in corners. All corners do not need roads.
7. Use Draw tools and the Color Palette to create rivers and bodies of water.
8. Use Arrow tool to resize and drag into position.
9. Use Text tool to label roads and bodies of water.
10. Add graphics.
11. Use Arrow tool to resize and drag into position.
12. Add a compass rose and a key.
13. Save. Name the map "Student Name Town."
14. Print and assemble the map.

Modifications

- Allow for a variety of compositions and maps based on individual student needs and skills.
- If graphics are not easily accessible, students can build structures using construction paper, Lego, or found materials, and then put the structures in position on their maps. Another alternative is using *Community Construction Kit*™ to create and add three-dimensional buildings.

Extensions

- Many different kinds of maps are possible using "North, South, East, or West?" as a guide. Encourage students to explore and try out mapping variations.
- Incorporate the mapping activity into language arts. Have students map out the setting in a novel. Give them the opportunity to identify the location in which a main character lives.
- Let students create an imaginary island.
- Use mapping for another location or historical period (e.g., a Medieval or Renaissance town, Roman Times or Ancient Egypt, or an Inuit settlement.)
- Have students make a map with written directions.
- Incorporate simulation software. Challenge students to trek across the American frontier in the mid-1800s. *Oregon Trail*® and *Oregon Trail II*™ allow students to problem solve in order to survive the arduous journey.

Mirror Images

Curricular Connections

Math/ Arts
- exploring and determining lines of symmetry
- constructing geometric models
- identifying transformations
- identifying two- and three-dimensional figures

Overview

Mirror, Mirror on the computer…"Mirror Images" introduces the fundamental elements necessary to create symmetrical objects on the computer. It also extends to another project — actually constructing the students' original symmetrical shapes. The computer drawing becomes the two-dimensional blueprint. "Mirror Images" is an opportunity for students to multi-task and experiment with the unique features of two different applications in order to generate a single document. The *AppleWorks*® Paint module allows for

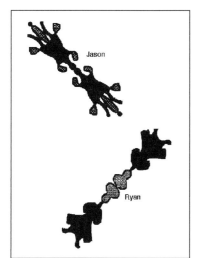

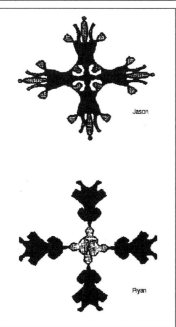

transformations and rotations necessary for symmetry. *Kid Pix Studio*™ *Deluxe* allows the user to automatically make perfect symmetry.

Cooperative Connection

Add a cooperative and synergistic dimension to this exercise. Group students into problem-solving pairs and pose the question, "How can text, graphics, or clip art be made symmetrical?" Answering this question gives students an opportunity for imaginative experimentation. Students work at the computer together to create several different answers to the question. Present the answers as "Mirror Images" in a Slide Show format. Self- and peer-assessment occur when all work is complete.

You could also involve all grades in the evaluation. Display the finished products of this cooperative activity in a continuous Slide Show on a computer in the school foyer. Place a comment sheet next to the computer so the entire school and visitors can participate in evaluating the Mirror Images Slide Show.

What to Do

• Because the instructions are based on two applications, the steps are divided into two sections, Making Mirror Images with *Kid Pix Studio*™ *Deluxe* and Transforming Mirror Images with *AppleWorks*®.
• Provide students with a hard copy of the instructions below and give a step-by-step demonstration.

Making Mirror Images with *Kid Pix Studio*™ *Deluxe*

1. Open a new document.
2. Use Wacky Brush tool with the Symmetry Option selected. Drag out a symmetrical image. (Tip: Start dragging from the middle of the screen towards the corners.)
3. Select the Moving Van tool. Use the Lasso Option to select the image.
4. Copy the image.
5. Type your name and Print one copy.
6. Saving is optional.

Transforming Images with *AppleWorks*®

1. Open a new *AppleWorks*® Paint document.
2. Go to the Edit menu and Paste the copied *Kid Pix* image.
3. Select the Paint Can. Choose *one solid* and *one pattern* to fill in some areas of the image. (Tip: Symmetry applies to color and pattern as well as shape. Not all areas need to be filled. Leave some white.)
3. Drag the Lasso tool around the entire image.
4. Go to the Edit menu and choose Copy.
5. Go to the Edit menu and choose Paste. (Tip: Make sure the Arrow is visible to move the pasted image away from the original image. If a correction is necessary, use the Undo function under the Edit menu *immediately!*)
6. While the second image is still selected, Transform or Rotate the image. Experiment!
7. Use the Arrow tool and move the rotated pattern. Place it on top of the original image so that the two images form a new symmetrical image.
8. Type your name. Save and Print one copy.

Modifications

- Encourage students who work quickly to try duplicating the symmetrical image and attaching it to the original image. Imagine the excitement when one student modifies their image into a more complicated design! Other students are bound to ask, "How did you do that?" Encourage peer teaching.
- Discuss the concept of designing an aesthetic image. Since the Wacky Brush enables the user to create perfectly symmetrical images, begin "Mirror Images" with *Kid Pix Studio*™ *Deluxe*. The symmetrical image is copied and pasted into an *AppleWorks*® Paint document where Transformations and Rotations are possible. Display the finished masterpieces in a classroom "Art Gallery"! Hard copies of each stage of the process from "Mirror Images" can be included in portfolios and discussed at a student-led conference.

Extensions

- The duplication process referred to in the first Modification is like *tiling* — filling a space with one design that has been "transformed." This technique is used by artists, such as M. C. Escher. Students can apply this duplicating activity to make a sheet of giftwrap. (Depending on the size of the gift, students may need to print multiple copies and tape them together.)
- Challenge students with some "What if...?" creative problem-solving. Once students have created their original works, ask them, "What if you had to construct a geometric model of your design as a three-dimensional figure?" Discuss aesthetics, the practical and logistical challenges of constructing the model, and possible materials and their potential strengths and weaknesses. Display samples of found materials and objects to stimulate imagination. Give students adequate time to try one of their ideas.
- Make the challenge described above multi-media. Capture the excitement of this "What if…" hands-on project with the digital or video camera. Display the models on a table in the "Art Gallery" with the digital pictures or the video presentation.

Multiply and Divide

Curricular Connections

Math
- multiplying and dividing
- demonstrating the properties of whole numbers
- relating division to multiplication
- interpreting problems visually and in words

Computer Connections

- using the text tool
- keyboarding
- using editing functions
- incorporating graphics
- designing a page layout

Software

- *Kid Pix Studio*™ *Deluxe*

Overview

Help students develop expertise in multiplication and division. "Multiply and Divide" is two separate yet complementary activities. However, the activities are interdependent because the multiplication and computer skills are fundamental to successful completion of the division segment. Each Part is intended to be a self-contained lesson, usually introduced at different times of the school year. Part One deals with multiplication. Part Two transfers the concepts and applies them to the division activity.

Using *Kid Pix Studio*™ *Deluxe*, students begin Part One by typing a multiplication problem in words. Based on the word problem their subsequent tasks are to:

- create a visual representation of the problem
- express the problem as a repeating addition sentence
- express the problem as a multiplication sentence

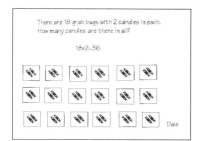

There are 18 grab bags with 2 candles in each. How many candles are there in all?

18x2=36

Dale

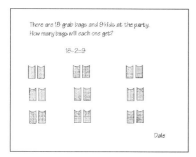

There are 18 grab bags and 9 kids at the party. How many bags will each one get?

18÷2=9

Dale

Tip: Consider using "Multiply and Divide" for student-led conferencing.

When all three tasks have been successfully completed, they are prepared for Division which is taught later. At that time, they open a new *Kid Pix Studio™ Deluxe* document and type a division problem in words. Based on the word problem their subsequent tasks are to:

- create a visual representation of the problem
- express the problem as a repeating subtraction sentence
- express the problem as a division sentence.

Cooperative Connection

Incorporate the use of math manipulatives. "Multiply and Divide" is a practical opportunity for teams to use cooperative strategies on and off computer. Begin with a simple exercise using the Number Family, such as 6, 5, 30, to express one multiplication problem and one division problem. Give students adequate time to practice using math manipulatives. The team applies 6, 5, 30 to different, but related, word problems. When each team demonstrates that they understand the concept, the team members take the manipulatives to the computer and continue the activity.

Consensus is crucial to any team decision. Each team agrees upon a Number Family and works cooperatively to type the word problems with the accompanying number sentences. The expectation is that the team incorporates elements of layout and design into its document. A self- and group-assessment guides them in developing a class presentation that includes an explanation and analysis of their process.

What to Do

- Give students a step-by-step demonstration using the Reproducible Master on page 66.
- Give each student a hard copy or send it electronically as a document over the network for the additional challenge of incorporating multi-tasking.

Modification

- Make "Multiply and Divide" socially interactive. Students work in pairs to compose a word problem and illustrate it. They print a copy and exchange it with another pair. The second pair completes the activity by adding the number sentences off computer.

Extension

- Confidence comes from repeating a familiar task. Repeat, reinforce, and integrate these math skills with other subjects such as language arts, science, social studies, or health. Once students are familiar with the process of "Multiply and Divide," compose math sentences based on topics in other subjects.

Multiplication

1. State the problem in words.

2. State the question as a multiplication question.

3. Show the problem using the drawing tools and/or the Rubber Stamp tool.

4. Type your name.

5. Save your work and print.

Division

1. State the problem in words.

2. State the question as a division question.

3. Show the problem using the drawing tools and/or the Rubber Stamp tool.

4. Type your name.

5. Save your work and print.

Computer Activities for the Cooperative Classroom by Linda M. Schwartz and Kathlene R. Willing

Geographic Elements

Overview

Precise questions combined with the use of spreadsheets stimulate students' interest in analyzing data and making comparisons. In "Geographic Elements," students compare their local environment to international cities using a spreadsheet to organize information, create graphs, and analyze data. They draw conclusions and write the analysis of their data in essay format. Five specific areas of investigation are included: Rainfall, Natural Vegetation, Soil, Natural Disasters, and Climatic Region. Other relevant categories may be added or substituted.

Together, students and teacher formulate a rubric based on the expectations of the analysis. Students develop spreadsheet expertise while researching information from both traditional and electronic sources. "Geographic Elements" combines learning the basic terminology and applying the practical spreadsheet skills — graphing included! By presenting the same information in different formats, students learn to analyze data from different perspectives and make comparisons. The finished product consists of spreadsheet, graph, and essay, which can be included in student portfolios.

Cooperative Connection

Use the cooperative learning Jigsaw technique developed by Kagan (1990). In this jigsaw, groups of students become "experts" in all aspects of a specific city. The number of groups is determined by the number of cities and the number of students in the class. Each Expert Group uses different resources to research the same five elements of the assigned city. To ensure consistency of information, the "experts" discuss which facts to communicate to the next group. They are then regrouped so that each group has one "expert" from each city. The task of the newly-formed cooperative group is to create one spreadsheet and enter the collective data. They also generate graphs based on the numerical data and analyze their research. The last cooperative group decision is how to creatively present their findings to the class.

What to Do

- Provide students with a hard copy of the following instructions and give a step-by-step demonstration.

Creating a Spreadsheet

1. Open a new *AppleWorks*® Spreadsheet document.
2. Go to File menu and choose Landscape orientation.
3. Go to Window menu and choose Page View.
4. Highlight all cells from A1 to F6.
5. Go to Format menu and choose Column Width. Increase to approximately 110 pts.
6. Go to Format menu and choose Row Height. Increase to approximately 60 pts.
7. Go to Format menu and choose Insert Header. Type the title of the spreadsheet. Type your name below the title.

Curricular Connections

Math/Language Arts/Social Studies and Teacher Productivity Tool
- developing research and communication skills
- formulating questions to gather and clarify data
- organizing information
- demonstrating an understanding of international cities
- analyzing, classifying, and interpreting information
- essay writing

Computer Connections
- creating and using spreadsheets
- entering data
- navigating between cells
- graphing
- searching electronic databases
- keyboarding

Software/Internet
- any spreadsheet application
- any integrated software package (*Microsoft Works*®, *AppleWorks*®)
- any word processing application
- any CD ROM atlas
- online encyclopedia(s) (*World Book, Britannica*)

Tip: This is an excellent opportunity to review essay writing and further develop keyboarding and word processing skills.

Geographic Elements
Taila

City / Element	Lima	Rome	Tokyo
Rainfall (July)	under 25 mm	25-50 mm	250-400 mm
Natural Vegetation	Tropical rainforest/tropical grassland	semi-desert: scrub/mixed forest	mixed forest
Soil	Tropical red soils, often lateritic	mountain soils: thin and stoney	tropical red soils, often lateritic
Natural Disasters	Deep ocean trenches	fold mountains	active volcanos, earthquakes, fold mountains
Climatic Region	Tropical: distinct wet and dry seasons	distinct wet and dry seasons	sub-tropical: humid

8. Enter categories in Column A. Enter cities in Row 1.
9. Enter information in remaining cells.
10. Highlight all cells. Go to Format menu and choose Alignment. Select Centre.
11. If text is more than one line, highlight the cell, go to Format menu and choose Alignment. Select Wrap.
12. Go to Options menu and choose Display. Select Solid Lines and deselect Column Headings and Row Headings.
13. Save.
14. Print page one only. Define the print range so excessive pages are not printed.

Creating a Graph

1. With the spreadsheet still in view, Highlight Rows 1 and 2 of the Spreadsheet.
2. Go to Options menu and choose Make Chart. Select Bar Graph. Select Axes and name the X and Y axes. (X = City, Y= Rainfall). Select Label and type the title (Rainfall). Deselect Legend. (Double click inside chart to make modifications.)
3. Resize the chart to fill the page leaving Rows 1 and 2 visible.
4. Save.
5. Print page one only. Define the print range so extra pages are not printed.

Modifications

- Have students create different graphs. Students examine the same data using different graph formats, (e.g., line, pie chart, scatter, area, or pictograph). Presenting the same information in various ways can clarify data. Select and print the graph that best represents the data. Students explain their choice of graph.
- Present the students with a Graph Challenge. Develop questions that require several rows of numerical data. Students create and analyze charts.

Extensions

- Help your students analyze scientific data. Students can apply the spreadsheet format and graphing to record and analyze scientific questions about states of matter, temperatures, or properties. For example, after recording their observations, students could analyze the temperatures at which various materials freeze or boil.
- Ask students to make a spreadsheet to chart their keyboarding progress. Keeping track of their speed and accuracy over a period of time will help them target areas for improvement.
- Invite students to use spreadsheets for making mathematical computations and calculations. The spreadsheet format allows them to apply formulae to many different numbers. They can change the data in some cells and observe the results. This kind of spreadsheet activity can be used as an estimating activity: Assign one column for an estimate and ask students to compare it with the value that appears in the answer column.
- Ask students to use a spreadsheet to develop a Pizza Party Budget! (If possible, hold the pizza party over a lunch period.)

DB City!

Curricular Connections

All Content Subject Areas and as a Teacher Productivity Tool
- developing research and communication skills
- formulating questions to gather and clarify data
- demonstrating an understanding of international cities
- sorting, analyzing and interpreting information
- drawing conclusions
- determining criteria for fields

Computer Connections

- creating a database
- searching a database
- sorting information
- creating fields and records
- navigating between fields
- keyboarding and entering data

Software/Internet

- any database application (*Filemaker® Pro*)
- any integrated software package (*Microsoft Works®, AppleWorks®*)
- any word processing application
- any CD ROM atlas
- online encyclopedia(s) (*World Book, Britannica*)

Did You Know? Every time we look up a phone number or the definition of a word or use an encyclopedia or CD ROM atlas, we are using a database.

Sorting — an outstanding benefit. "DB City" combines the acquisition of database terminology — file, record, and field, with the application of practical skills — sorting included! Information from various fields in the database can be juxtaposed and analyzed.

Overview

"DB City" is an excellent activity for introducing databases. Students get practical experience in building, using, and manipulating databases about different cities. They use the information in their databases to analyze and compare statistics.

Introduce the idea of a computer database by expanding the spreadsheet concept in "Geographic Elements." Like a spreadsheet, a database enables students to analyze data. However, databases are more flexible. Not only do they hold a greater volume of information that is readily accessible, they can be added to, changed, or updated at any time. What makes the database unique? It's archival — save it for next year! Databases can be used indefinitely. One class may create it and another class use it for research.

Cooperative Connection

In this activity, students design a database and research the information to enter into the database. Then they work in small groups to analyze the information for a Simulation/Debate. The students tackle the question, "Which is the best city to host the next Olympic Games?" The question will ultimately be resolved by debate based on an analysis of facts in their databases.

What to Do

About Databases in General

Database applications are unique, but they all follow the same basic principles. The user creates "Fields" and enters information to create "Records." Once fields are created, data entry is possible. Most applications allow the user to create multiple layouts and design customized printed reports. Depending on the database application, students may have to determine the fields and design the layout before going to the computer.

Start Building the Database

Information in the "Geographic Elements" spreadsheet becomes the foundation for an International City database. City is the first "Field" because it defines the "Record." The other fields are: Rainfall, Natural Vegetation, Soil, Natural Disasters, and Climatic Region. Broaden the scope of the database with other relevant fields, such as population, location, famous people, and land forms. When the fields have been determined, students enter their research as single words or concise phrases. When all information has been entered, students can formulate questions to initiate searches. You can start them off by asking, "Which cities have been hit by earthquakes?" This is an opportune time to teach (or review) search techniques using attributes or "Key Words." Students discover answers by entering the most likely Key Word — "earthquake." Ask the question again, with slightly narrowed search criteria: "Which *South American* cities have been hit by earthquakes?" (Students use a "Boolean Search" technique, entering "earthquake AND South America.") The search is repeated by replacing South America with other locations.

Tip: Databases are versatile teacher tools! Teachers can use a database to make labels, write report cards, map out curriculum, and create templates to design brochures, newspapers, or newsletters.

Conducting the Activity

Arrange the students in small groups to role play members of subcommittees of the International Olympic Committee (IOC). The groups will be deciding which city should host the next Olympic Games. The students will research different cities and create databases with information they gather. To ensure broad representation, groups should submit a list of 10–12 potential cities for approval from the IOC Director (teacher). When the Director has approved their selections, the students design the database.

Have the groups define the fields for their database. As part of the cooperative process, each group should also brainstorm a list of questions that will be used to query the database. Together, they analyze their data, and come to a conclusion about the next host city. Diverse opinions will result in spirited debate. Video-taped debates can be incorporated into the group and self-evaluations. The process ends with each group's selecting the host city.

Each group member writes an essay to summarize their conclusions. This presents another opportunity to practice essay writing and to continue building keyboarding and word processing skills in combination with a database. Any or all of the work in this activity can be included in student portfolios.

Setting Up the Database

Tip: These four-part instructions use the Database module of *AppleWorks*®. If using another database application provide students with appropriate instructions.

1. Open a new *AppleWorks*® Database. A "Define Database Fields" window appears.
2. Type the name of the field in "Field Name." Select "Field Type." Use the default setting, "Text" unless it is a numerical field that will be calculated.
3. Select "Create." The first field is defined.
4. Type the name of the next field in "Field Name."
5. Repeat Steps 2 and 3 until all the fields are entered.
6. Select "Done."
7. Enter data into the field boxes. Use the Tab Key to move to the next field.
8. When data has been entered into all of the fields, create a "New Record." Go to the Edit menu and choose New Record.
9. Repeat Steps 2–9 until all Records have been entered.
10. This Entry Layout is for entering data.
11. Save.

Searching the Database

Tip: Searches are most efficiently done using the Entry Layout.

1. Go to the Layout menu and choose Find.
2. Select the field and type the "key word."
3. Go to the left sidebar and choose Find.
4. Those records with the key word are now visible.
5. To return to all records, go to the Organize menu and choose Show All Records.
6. To find a record with a specific number, go to the left sidebar and choose the Record Book tab. Scroll down to the desired record.

Creating a New Layout

1. Go to Layout menu and choose New Layout.
2. Name the Layout and make a selection for the type of layout desired.
3. In the Set Field Order window, choose a field from the left side and select Move so that it appears on the right side of the window.
4. Repeat Step 3 for all the fields you wish you to move.
5. Select OK when done.
6. Save.

Customizing a Layout

1. Go to Layout menu and choose Layout.
2. Rearrange the text boxes and field names by dragging.
3. Use the drawing tools to enhance the appearance.
4. When the layout is complete, go to Layout menu and choose Browse.
5. Save.

Modifications

- Provide a broad range of questions. Include questions that require simple factual answers.
- Pose questions that challenge Higher Order Thinking Skills.
- Develop a rubric with students to guide them in formulating the questions.
- Vary the number of cities in the database.

Extensions

- Use the Reading Buddies model and set up a system of Database Buddies. Pair older students with younger ones. Older students create the database on a topic being studied by the younger ones and teach them how to enter, search, and sort information.
- Use any subject, any topic. Databases are created to store information. The list of subjects is endless: animals, provinces/states, people, novel studies, scientific experiments, reading lists, library catalogues, materials for building structures, soils, vehicles.

Power Puzzles

Curricular Connections

Science
- reinforcing scientific terminology
- organizing information
- reviewing notes
- composing definitions
- communicating information

Computer Connections
- creating and formatting spreadsheets
- adding color to cells
- using text boxes to enter data
- navigating between cells

Software/Internet
- any spreadsheet application
- any integrated software package (*Microsoft Works*®, *AppleWorks*®)

Overview

Extend students' skills by applying the basic principles of a spreadsheet in this challenging activity.

"Power Puzzles" generates the spark to reinforce terminology. We have selected "electricity" as our topic. Substitute any topic and "start the engines" by brainstorming the relevant vocabulary.

Students independently select a minimum number of words from the brainstormed list. They study their notes and textbooks in order to compose concise clues for each word. Once the clues are written, students arrange the puzzle words on graph paper so all words connect in at least one place. When words and clues have been arranged, students apply the layout to a computer spreadsheet. Students should save two versions of "Power Puzzles" — one with the answers and one without.

Power Puzzle

	A	B	C	D	E	F	G	H	I	J
1										
2										
3										
4										
5										
6										
7										
8										
9										
10										
11										
12										
13										
14										
15										
16										

Across

1-B ocean water level according to the position of the moon

3-A able to float

6-G festival that honours ancestors

7-F _____ spills pollute the ocean

9-A people who work against their will

9-H traditional Japanese hot drink

13-D "Long, long _____"

15-C Nature's force

Down

A-9 Japan's main religion

B-1 giant wave caused by volcanic action or earthquakes

C-9 festival that includes a parade

D-3 ancient art of meditating

E-9 record of the oceans' sound waves showing the shape of the ocean floor

F-1 particles that make up the beach

H-4 a person who destroys something that's already there

J-1 the study of oceans

Tip: The number of words in each puzzle determines the overall size of the spreadsheet and the size of the cells!

Print multiple blank puzzles for students to exchange. Print one copy of the answers and place it in a "Power Puzzles" folder with two pockets. Make the folder accessible so students can check their answers. Place blank puzzles in the other pocket for next year. Include "Power Puzzles" in student portfolios.

Cooperative Connection

In our electricity-focused example, students could study inventors, make calculations using electrical units of measurement, and conduct electrical experiments to develop vocabulary for integrated puzzles. Students work in teams, and each team takes an "electrical name" (e.g., Spark-plugs). They each brainstorm a different electricity-related topic to develop vocabulary for the puzzle. Selecting a minimum number of words, the team uses their notes and textbooks to compose the clues. When clues are written and words connected, the team creates the spreadsheet on computer. It is saved and two versions are printed. The answer sheet is placed in the "Power Puzzles" folder.

What to Do

• In the examples we discussed above, we chose "electricity" as our topic. Specific instructions are not included here because the words and the way in which they will be connected are unique to each "Power Puzzle." Refer to "What to Do" in "Geographic Elements," page 67. Use those instructions as a guide for creating the "Power Puzzles" spreadsheets.

• In general, students will:
  – arrange words on graph paper
  – count grid boxes across and down to determine the size of the spreadsheet
  – highlight that number of cells across and cells down on the spreadsheet
  – adjust Column Width and Row Height, repeat adjustment if necessary, leaving ample space for clues
  – enter words in the spreadsheet
  – select and fill empty cells with black from the Color Palette.

Modifications

• Enhance the puzzles' visual appearance by adding graphics.

• Emphasize the positive. Make it synergistic by combining the strengths of individual students. Create teams to develop a puzzle that reflects the distinct talents of each team member.

• Add an element of competition to a cooperative game. Challenge teams to "beat the clock" in solving a "Power Puzzle." Use a spreadsheet to create a matrix with team names and puzzle names. Post the matrix for teams to track their speed in completing the different puzzles.

Extensions

• Use "Power Puzzles" for topics that are often neglected when considering computer integration — health and physical education, art, music, drama, and other languages. You can create and compile an inventory of crossword puzzles in any subject.

• Use a different approach to solve the same problem: Create "Power Puzzles" in an *AppleWorks*® Draw environment using the Spreadsheet tool. Spreadsheets, like drawing tools and text boxes, can be dragged out, resized, moved, and locked. Explain that computer tasks can be accomplished using

Integrated Activities — Grades Five and Six

different techniques. Give students the opportunity to experiment with alternative methods for completing an activity.

Internet Ideas

- Find puzzle vocabulary on the Internet. For this electricity-related activity, students can check out the Theatre of Electricity at the Museum of Science, Boston.
  http://www.mos.org/sln/toe/toe.html
- Explore Science Centres around the world. Give students time to take virtual trips to outstanding international science centres. This Web site is the umbrella organization that lists over 400 science centers worldwide. Create other science "Power Puzzles" using information gathered from different centres.
  http://www.tryscience.org/fieldTripFASC.html
- For explanations of puzzling science terms, ask *Bill Nye, the Science Guy*:
  http://www.billnye.com/openNyelabs.html

Hypermedia Bicycle Tour

Curricular Connections

Spanish, French, German, or any other language
- speaking and writing in the language
- reading and researching
- summary writing
- note taking
- reading maps
- communicating information

Computer Connections

- using hypermedia software
- keyboarding
- importing media

Software/Internet

- *HyperStudio®*
- *HyperCard®*
- any hypermedia authoring tool

Overview

This activity assumes that students have basic knowledge of *HyperStudio®*.

In "Hypermedia Bicycle Tour," students present an animated tour in the language of the country they are studying. They mesh three fundamental elements — knowledge of the language, research of the country, and computer skills. Evaluation for this activity should focus equally on all three elements. This is an ideal project to include in their Electronic Portfolios and for student-led conferences.

Students use *HyperStudio®* application to bring it all together. They enliven the presentation with animation, digital photos, video and audio clips, *QuickTime* movies, or Internet graphics and links. Each student develops a stack of five cards to represent a different part of the country. For a tour of the entire country, link all stacks.

Cooperative Connection

Hold a Hypermedia Grand Tour Conference. The Grand Tour integrates a broad range of knowledge and skills. A conference model presents a practical opportunity for students to speak the language they are studying and offers numerous opportunities for computer use:

- *database* – to generate name tags for delegates
- *spreadsheet* – to track committee progress and plan menus and budgets
- *desktop publishing* – to create posters, flyers, invitations, programs, and travel brochures
- *word processing* – to write narration (script) and to create an evaluation form
- *Internet* – to download music and graphics
- *draw or paint program* – to decorate the room with banners and art work

In the plenary session, all tour guides present their stacks to each other. Students form teams in the next session. Each team forms a committee responsible for one aspect of the final presentation:

- *tour route* – determines the order in which the stacks are linked
- *music* – selects background music for the tour
- *narration* – provides a narrative of the tour
- *program* – creates the program for the audience
- *advertising* – creates posters, flyers or invitations
- *food* – plans and budgets the menu and decor
- *evaluation* – formulates an evaluation form for audience feedback

What to Do

Storyboarding for Hypermedia

Apply this familiar approach to a different task. Use five standard file cards to represent the five cards in the *HyperStudio*® stack. The stack opens with a menu card that is linked to a culture card, a major cities card, a tourist attractions card, and an industry/agriculture card.

Each student extracts the relevant information from their research and writes the synopsis for each card on separate sheets of paper. They then design each card to show the layout of the written synopsis, the visual features they plan to use, and the buttons (links to each card). The menu card has four buttons which allow the viewer to navigate through the stack. The other cards have at least one button that links back to the menu. Enjoy the tour and the students' enthusiasm!

Conducting the Activity

Provide students with a copy of the instructions on page 75.

Modification

- Allow for a range of complexity in the stacks to accommodate individual student needs and skills.

Extensions

- Use the Grand Tour Method as a new approach to book reports. Students take individual chapters and present a Grand Tour of the novel.
- Relive historical times with your class. Invite them to create a tour of the development of a colony, settlement, or country; to follow the discoveries of the explorers in the New World; or to guide the audience through Ancient Egypt, Greece, or Rome.

Internet Idea

- Encourage your students to be virtual explorers. They can follow the expeditions of *National Geographic* explorers online and communicate with them by e-mail. Suggest they use the *Trek Viewer* to examine a detailed map of the journey, or learn about *Explorers in Residence*. http://www.nationalgeographic.com/

Tip: No surprises! Establish expectations before students begin their stacks. Develop criteria for the rubric together. After the Grand Tour has been presented, teams read and analyze the results of the evaluation.

Student Instructions for Hypermedia Presentations

1. Open *Hyperstudio*™ and select New Stack. Do not change the card size. *Save often!*

2. Create six cards, five for the stack and one for a working card. Go to the Edit menu and choose New Card. Repeat five more times.

3. Go to Tools menu and drag down the Tools Palette. Go to Colors menu and drag down the Colors Palette. Place both beside the card.

4. While on the sixth card, choose the Text painting tool "T" from the Tools Palette and type "working card." This is to be used for creating and modifying graphics and clip art. It will be deleted when the stack is finished.

5. Go to Move menu to return to the first card. Move menu is also used to go to other cards.

6. Using the Tools and Colors Palettes create and arrange graphics, painted text and visible buttons for Card 1, Menu. Visible buttons are included for design purposes. You will link the buttons when all cards are completed. Painted text is "glued" onto the background and *cannot be manipulated or linked!*

7. To create blocks of text that can be manipulated or linked, go to Objects menu and choose Text Object. Hypertext Links may also be created using the Objects menu.

8. Make selections for clip art on Card 6. To do this, go to File menu and select Add Clip Art from Disk File. Select the appropriate clip art and place on Card 6. Clip art may also be imported from other sources to Card 6. Encourage students to create their own clip art on this card, as well. Use the Effects option from the Edit menu to add interesting details to the art.

9. Use Card 6 as a working card to resize, modify or make the clip art into a Graphic Object. Copy and paste on to Card 1.

10. Incorporate some, but not necessarily all, of the following special features somewhere in the stack.
    - Use the Add Clip Art option to add video clips or digital photos.
    - Go to the Objects menu and choose Add a Button to add sound, *QuickTime* movies, or New Button Actions.

11. When the design of Card 1 is complete, move to Card 2. Repeat Steps 6–10. Repeat for all remaining cards.

12. When all cards are completed, go to Extras menu and choose Storyboard to see an overview of the stack. If changes are not necessary, select Card 6 (the working card) and Delete it.

13. Link the buttons. Start with the Menu card. When linking other cards, consider giving the viewer the option of going directly to another card, back to the Menu card, or both.

Computer Activities for the Cooperative Classroom by Linda M. Schwartz and Kathlene R. Willing

Science Fair

Curricular Connections

Science/Math/Language Arts
• reading and researching
• note taking
• constructing scientific models
• conducting experiments
• communicating information

Computer Connections
• using presentation software
• importing media

Software/Internet
• *Microsoft Power Point*®
• *Mpower*™
• *MP Express*™

Tip: Make students stakeholders. Evaluation can be a cooperative initiative involving students in assessing both the process and the product.

Overview

Toss out the poster boards and present science projects in a new medium! "Science Fair" uses the presentation tool, *Microsoft Power Point*®, to add dazzle to science projects. Students choose a topic and research their projects using a combination of traditional and electronic sources. They may conduct scientific experiments, examine scientific theories, and/or construct models.

When the research is complete, they create a complementary 15–20 minute, *Microsoft Power Point*® presentation. "Science Fair" is based on the assumption that students have basic knowledge of *Microsoft Power Point*®. Bulleted summaries, well designed screens, and engaging features, such as clip art, photos, animation, sound, and links to the Internet, are elements for maintaining audience attention. Students should display the experiment and construction model during their *Microsoft Power Point*® presentation.

Together, you and the students create the criteria and the tools for assessment of their projects. This presentation can be included in their Electronic Portfolios for student-led conferences.

Cooperative Connection

Don't have just another Science Fair, make it a Science Symposium, where scientific experts present their combined research. The partners research the topic independently and meet regularly to discuss their findings. They blend their ideas, solve problems, and plan their next step. Cooperatively, they conduct the necessary experiments and/or construct the requisite models. They develop an outline of what to present and a strategy for presentation. Together they create a *Power Point*® presentation to be delivered at the Symposium. In preparation for the presentation, the pair composes and rehearses their speech. The scientific team devises a plan to encourage audience participation as well as an evaluation form for audience feedback.

What to Do

• Provide students with a copy of the instructions, Creating a *Power Point*® Presentation, on page 77. Although the steps are few, the process is long. Remind them to save often.

Modification

• Accommodate individual students by modifying the degree of research and the sophistication of the presentations.

Extension

• Use the Symposium setting for other events such as a Young Authors' Conference, a United Nations Day, or an Young Artists' Exposition.

Creating a *Power Point*® Presentation

1. Open a new *Power Point*® document. Choose a design layout.

2. Select Screen View.

3. Click in the text boxes to add titles, subtitles, and information.

4. Go to Insert menu to add Word Art, Clip Art, Photos from Files, Charts, Movies, Hyperlinks, or Sounds.

5. Go to Insert menu to insert a New Slide.

6. Go to File menu and choose Save.

7. Repeat Steps 3–6 for each new slide.

8. Go to Slide Sorter View to look at all slides or to change the order of slides.

9. Go to Slide Show View to preview the slide show and see how it works.

10. Save.

Computer Activities for the Cooperative Classroom by Linda M. Schwartz and Kathlene R. Willing

Children and War — A WebQuest

Suggested Novels About World War II

• *Spying on Miss Muller* by Eve Bunting
• *Dawn of Fear* by Susan Cooper
• *Too Young to Fight* by Priscilla Galloway
• *Daniel's Story* by Carol Matas
• *The Cook Camp* by Gary Paulson
• *The Sky Is Falling* by Kit Pearson
• *Return to Topaz* by Yoshio Ukeda
• *Devil's Arithmetic* by Jane Yolen
• *Hiroshima* by Lawrence Yep

Tip: Check a selected list of World War II Middle School Literature and Resources at this Web site: http://www.weymouthsis.org/~library/ww2.html

Tip: Select from many options for cooperative presentation: video or radio broadcast, documentary, newscast, or game show. Incorporate individual and group evaluation to equally assess analysis and presentation.

Overview

Add immediacy and relevance to an historic novel study by integrating it with a WebQuest. Encourage students to utilize Internet resources for researching background information. "Children and War" develops empathy, understanding, and social conscience. For an in-depth description of WebQuests, see Chapter 6, page 104.

World War II made a deep impact on the lives of the children who lived through it. These impressions have been documented in a rich body of literature, films, paintings, photographs, and Internet sites. In "Children and War — A Webquest," students read an historical novel based on World War II.

After students have read and studied a novel, they embark on a WebQuest as newspaper reporters. Their task is to find answers to specific questions about the effects of war on children. Each student then writes a newspaper article synthesizing the novel and the WebQuest research. The articles may be reproduced in newspaper format using desktop publishing. Students can research the appearance of World War II newspapers and use techniques to make them appear historical. They may enhance the newspaper with other editorial features relevant to the historical times. A single copy of the article can be included in a student's portfolio.

Important: Allow several sessions for students to complete the WebQuest.

Cooperative Connection

Students work with a WebQuest partner. They can both read the same novel, or they may read different novels, and then work with each other. Reading different novels broadens the scope of the project because it allows for contrasts and comparisons. When the WebQuest is complete, several groups of students collaborate and choose to make a presentation in one of three ways:

• *Video-taped Drama* – Several partners combine their research into a collaborative script. The class views their video taped production.
• *Radio Broadcast* – Several groups collaborate on a script, which is then aired for the class.
• *Newspaper* – Several partners work cooperatively to combine their ideas. They use a desktop publishing application to produce a newspaper which is read by the class.

Part of the cooperative process is for students to compile a list of jobs necessary for each type of presentation. They cooperatively assign the jobs and fulfill their designated responsibilities. For their presentation, they must decide as a group, how they will present and what each individual's responsibilities are.

What to Do

• Either retype (or scan) "Children and War — A WebQuest" into a word processing document. If the word processing application allows hot links (Chapter 6, page 105), students can use the electronic document to access the Internet directly. If hot links are not available, print out a hard copy of the WebQuest or use the Reproducible Master on page 79 to make copies.

Children and War — A WebQuest

Description

You are a news reporter for an international media outlet. You have been sent to do a story on the impact of war on children.

Task

You may choose to write a story for a current day newspaper or a World War II newspaper.

Resources

The following Web sites will help you in your search.
- Save the Children: http://193.129.255.93/childrights/index.html
- UN Convention on the Rights of the Child: http://www.oneworld.org/childrights/convention.html
- Voices of Youth: Children in War: http://www.unicef.org/voy/meeting/war/warpics.html
  http://www.unicef.org/voy/meeting/war/warphoto.html
- What did you do in the War Grandma? An oral history project:
  http://www.stgbrown.edu/projects/wwII_women/tocCS.html

Process

Visit each of the Web sites listed above. Open a word processing document and multi-task to take notes on the information you find to help you answer the following questions.

- How are children and their families affected by war?
- In what ways does war interfere with daily life?
- What are the effects of war?
- What did some people do during the war?
- What are the rights of children?
- Why are rights important to children?

Advice

The notes you take are to be used for your newspaper article. Format your word processing document into three pages. Page one to answer the questions, page two to take notes, and page three to write your newspaper article.

Evaluation

Your evaluation will be based on answers to the questions, notes taken from the resources, and your newspaper article. The criteria will be to:

- demonstrate an understanding of the impact of war on children
- demonstrate an understanding of the rights of children
- describe the effect the war has on the lives of children and their families
- analyze, synthesize, and interpret diverse information
- use appropriate vocabulary

Conclusion

You should now be an expert on Children and War. Write a personal response to the information that you gathered from the Internet for this WebQuest. Type this response in a new word processing document.

Computer Activities for the Cooperative Classroom by Linda M. Schwartz and Kathlene R. Willing

- Begin a discussion with the students, inviting their ideas about the impact of war on children. Present an overview of how they will read novels, use the Internet, write an article, and do a group presentation. You may find it useful to summarize the points on a student handout, or in an electronic file they can access easily.
- Arrange to have the students read and discuss their novels. When students are ready to go on the Internet, review the details of the document "War and Children — A WebQuest." Make sure that students have a hard copy if the file is not available on the computer. They need the web addresses on file so they can multi-task to cut and paste them.
- Discuss the evaluation criteria with your class. Make sure they are posted on the computer and/or somewhere in the classroom. You may also want to provide a hard copy, which students can take home.

Modification

- Change the nature of the questions so that the answers require more or less detail and depth. Add more questions. Pair students so that their strengths complement each other and their individual needs are accommodated.

Extensions and Internet Ideas

- Showcase student work on a Web page. Students create a Web page based on their research for "Children and War — A WebQuest." Several Web design applications are available to create Web pages, such as *Macromedia® Dreamweaver™*, *Web Workshop™PRO*, *Sarah's Page Web Builder©* and *Microsoft FrontPage®*. There are several options available for publishing the page on the Web:
  - It can be added to the school's Web site.
  - Some software companies, such as *Sunburst*, offer free publishing on their Web site if using their software.
  - YAHOO!® *Geocities* http://geocities.yahoo.com/ permits free creation and publication of Web sites.
  - Search the Web for other sites that offer this service using a phrase, such as "publish educational Web site."
  - ThinkQuest Junior http://www.advanced.org/thinkquestjr.html is an online contest in which students create an entry that showcases what they have learned in any subject. The Web pages in this site are designed by students for students. Refer to the Extensions in "What Was It Like Then?" Chapter 4.

5   Implementing a Cooperative Medieval Unit

Integrating Cooperative Learning, Computer Skills, and Design Technology

Using the principles of cooperative learning addressed in Chapter One, two teachers successfully meshed cooperative learning, computers, and design technology in a Grade Four Medieval Unit. This chapter describes that process. The classroom teacher was eager to take a cross-curricular approach, but she felt overwhelmed by the prospect of simultaneously introducing a number of other new ideas in April. Collaboration and team teaching with the Computer Resource Teacher made the project less stressful and cushioned that critical "first step in the journey."

After researching and immersing themselves for several weeks in the life and times of people during the Medieval Period, the students' culminating activity was to design and build an abbey. The focus was to teach students cooperative skills by having them design the abbey on the computer and ultimately build it in the classroom.

In the initial stage of the project, the students used the computer to design a bird's-eye view of an abbey. The students used *Kid Pix Studio™ Deluxe,* because it is open-ended and it incorporates both paint and text. In the second stage of the project, students worked in groups of four to cooperatively select one design, which eventually became the group's blueprint for building the abbey.

Choosing a Design: A Cooperative Approach

The teacher deliberately placed the students into a problematic situation where cooperative skills were essential. Since each group was faced with the challenge of peacefully choosing a design, this was the appropriate time to introduce the principles of working cooperatively to solve a problem. Their solutions evolved as the result of their exposure to the elements of cooperative learning. Students from all groups were assembled for a cooperative learning orientation. Two main goals were outlined. The first was academic — to understand the architecture of the abbey in order to design a bird's-eye view and to construct the model. The second goal was social — to learn the process for working cooperatively by assuming the various roles.

Students were told that since they had already developed their individual designs, they and the teacher would work through a process to help them cooperatively select one design that they would use for their model.

The teacher selected four key roles for the Grade Fours' first attempt at cooperative learning —*facilitator, timekeeper, questioner,* and *supporter.* The students familiarized themselves with the roles. As the students worked together on the project, they focused on different interaction skills to help them understand the roles and how to use them positively to work towards their common goal. Using the Individual/Group Self-Assessment, the students reflected on their own participation as well as the group's. They entered check marks for the skills that applied to them and their group. They had the option to make comments in the last column. (Note the student sample below. You will find the Reproducible Master "Individual/ Group Self-Assessment" on page 18.)

Individual/Group Self-Assessment

Student Name __Temma P__

Social Skill	Myself	Group	Comments
FACILITATOR			
Staying on task	✔	✔	
Taking turns equally		✔	
TIMEKEEPER			
Pacing group work	✔	✔	
Watching the time			
QUESTIONER			
Asking for help or clarification	1/2	✔	
Asking useful questions	✔	✔	
Contributing ideas	✔	✔	
SUPPORTER			
Sharing materials	✔	✔	
Expressing support/praising	1/2	✔	
Being courteous	✔	✔	
Being self-controlled		✔	
Using quiet voices	✔	✔	
Including everyone	✔	✔	

The first task at hand was to model a Social Interaction Skill with the class. Using a Y-chart, the teacher elicited ideas to demonstrate what active listening looked like and sounded like. (See the Y-chart on page 19.)

Since each student had drawn a computer version of a bird's-eye view of an abbey, each group had to decide which plan they would use as a blueprint for construction. Knowing that this could put some students in a very vulnerable situation, the teacher set the stage for the group work. She described four strategies for arriving at a decision: compromise, consensus, majority rule, and disagreeing agreeably. Students understood that it was acceptable to use any or all of these strategies as they worked in their groups.

The students brainstormed a T-chart about disagreeing agreeably (see page 22). Next, the teacher led a discussion outlining the relevant criteria for reviewing their own and others' designs. Students also discussed the process of working together and developed criteria for evaluation. Their task was to observe how the group came to decisions and how they worked together. At the end of the project, they would share their findings with the class and evaluate their process. The purpose of the lesson was to get students thinking about and using supportive and diplomatic language with each other.

Criteria were established for individual and group evaluations to ensure that the roles of timekeeper, questioner, supporter, and facilitator would be practiced. An Individual/Group Self-Assessment Sheet was designed based on the following key ideas:

- Did I say something I liked about my own design? Did I give the reason why?
- Did every member of the group say something positive about another person's design? Did we give the reason why?
- Did I facilitate to make certain that everyone's work was included?
- Did others make certain that everyone's work was included?
- Was I aware of the time and did I keep on task?
- Did I ask useful questions to clarify and contribute to the discussion?

The groups of four worked together for twenty minutes and then presented their choice to the class. Students were able to resolve conflicts that arose because the groundwork had been clearly established. They cooperatively selected a design and developed it so that each person in their group could accept it. It is interesting to note that each of the designs synthesized the groups' collective ideas. Everyone felt positive about the final design. When they completed the selection process, each member filled out an Individual/Group Self-Assessment. This initial assessment was then used as the teaching tool and model for the discussion focus in the next session.

The teacher created an electronic folder containing all four design documents. This gave students the option of using elements from each document to create the final design. Decisions about the design were then taken to the computer for students to create the final blueprint. Using one computer, the four students worked cooperatively to select, copy, and paste the necessary parts of each design into the new document. Supportive discussion ensued about the techniques of selecting, copying, and pasting; which part of the design to capture and transfer; the refinements necessary to synthesize all components; and how to blend the components into a single, cohesive design. When students printed the final blueprint, they each filled out another Individual/Group Self-Assessment and discussed it with their group.

With the foundation for social skills and the design process complete, the next session addressed the construction of the abbey. The session started with the teacher demonstrating how to make structures out of recycled greeting cards. She provided each group with a cardboard base and assembled craft materials for students to use for their abbeys. During the construction sessions, the groups worked together and pointed out positive contributions. Various methods of ongoing verbal and written evaluation were incorporated and used within the group and with the class.

Each group presented their abbey to the class at the end of the building phase. Group members explained their individual contribution to the project as well as talking about the process of working together. Their final evaluation consisted of a group assessment and a personal reflection that was shared with the whole class.

Final Assessment

Group reflections on the process:

- Overall, how did our group work together?
- What strengths did our group demonstrate?
- What difficulties did we face as a group?
- How did we resolve difficulties as a group?
- Was our conflict resolution successful? Why or why not?
- What did we learn by working together?
- Suggestions or comments for future projects.

Personal reflections on the process:

- I felt good about...
- In the future, I will try to improve...
- The next time I work as part of a group, I...

Extensions

The Medieval Unit serves as a model for any type of cooperative project in which students will be working in small groups, and it proves that one can begin teaching cooperative skills at any time during the year — even in April!

Use the Medieval Unit as a model for other subject areas; for example, in science, to design a city in space, an exotic animal zoo, or an authentic animal habitat. For social studies, students might design a new park or redesign their school playground. The blueprints could be generated on or off the computer. These projects can also incorporate mathematics by having the students measure to scale or create their own scale.

Other ideas can be built around the design process to accommodate different computer and communication skills. In groups, students could design a survey that requires interviewing. To simulate a real-life situation, each group could be a competing company that has to promote an idea to the community. Each group would make a presentation using multi-media software, such as *Microsoft® Power Point®* or *HyperStudio™*. The students would format the survey on computer, gather and enter the data, and create spreadsheets and graphs to analyze the results. With some thought and planning, computers and cooperative learning can be integrated into most curriculum subjects.

6 How to Integrate the Internet into the Curriculum

by Sandra Mingail*

Tis true: there's magic in the web of it.

William Shakespeare,
Othello: Act 3, Scene 4,

Introduction to the Internet

Once bitten by the Internet bug, there is no turning back. There is something magnetic about this technology — an invisible force that connects the user to a global community of information seekers, learners, and teachers. It is an engaging, interactive medium where one click of the mouse launches the user into an irresistible journey of learning.

Of course, simply logging on to the Internet will not instantly transform students into stellar academic achievers. Nor will it make the job any easier for teachers. But when incorporating use of the Internet in the classroom, students are exposed to a virtual treasure trove of learning resources and experiences.

"Is it difficult to integrate Internet use into existing lesson plans?" has an easy answer. "Not really." It does, however, require a subtle paradigm shift. Rather than assigning specific textbook pages to read, challenge students to visit designated Web sites to find current news, information, and statistics. Turn a novel study into an e-mail interview opportunity with the book's author, or an online debate with another class studying the same work. Enliven an animal unit with a virtual visit to the San Diego Zoo. Whet students' appetites for an art project with a no-cost online field trip to the Louvre.

Internet use enables students to search, retrieve, collect, and exchange information. It allows them to collaborate with peers across the ocean. It lets them communicate with subject experts in both the academic and work worlds. More importantly, with proper guidance, classroom-based Internet use helps students develop critical and analytical skills. It lays the foundation to both educational and workplace success in the new information-based society. This pervasive new technology puts the power of lifelong learning into students' hands.

Bolster Professional Development Join an educator's mailing list, subscribe to educational e-newsletters, or enrol in a Web-based tutorial. Thousands of lesson plans, supplemental resources, and reproducible materials are shared online by teachers around the world. In listservs, teachers exchange lesson plans and collaborate on group projects.

---

* A special thank you to Sandra Mingail for her contribution to our book. Ms. Mingail brings a combination of her communications and education degrees and twenty years of experience in the media and training industries to this chapter. Her syndicated online column, *familycompute.com*, teaches Web literacy skills to parents and children. Sandra is Vice President of New Media for Humansense.com.

About This Chapter

There are seven key concepts in this chapter. Each concept is developed in a separate section of the chapter. All seven of these key concepts are essential to effective Internet use.

The sections begin with an "Internet Vocabulary Builder" and a brief topic summary. All seven key concept sections include a "Student Internet Activity," and a related "Go Surf" Web site. The activities allow for both independent exploration and cooperative group work. They include reproducible materials that students can collect in a personal Student Internet Reference Folder.

Create Student Internet Reference Folders. Prepare a reference folder for each student that contains this chapter's reproducible materials. If they have a question when they are using the Internet independently, they can refer to their folders first. If their folders don't have the answer, students can ask the teacher and/or peers for help.

The Seven Key Concepts	
Section	**Key Concept**
1 The ABCs of the Internet	– describes what the Internet is and how it works
2 Make Friends With Your Browser	– details the basics of browser software that gives the user access to the information highway
3 You Be the Judge	– outlines how to evaluate sites and provides criteria for judging their value
4 Finding What You Want	– provides search engine strategies for sifting through the vast amount of online information
5 Communicating With Others	– focuses on how to use electronic mail, the most popular method of communication on the Internet
6 Respecting the Work of Others	– explores ethical issues of Internet use, such as copying, printing, and downloading other people's files and programs
7 WebQuests	– presents a flexible learning model where students go online in search of answers

On the surface, the Internet is a vast collection of machines and cables. Below the surface, it is a living, vibrant network that empowers students to discover the joy of learning, together. It is a global community of people who share constantly expanding resources.

The World Wide Web — commonly referred to as the "Web" — is a subset of the Internet. It is a multi-media service that mixes graphics, text, images, video, animation, and sound. Other subsets of the Internet include information transfer, such as Telnet and File Transfer Protocol (FTP).

Section 1   The ABCs of the Internet

Learning the ABCs of the Internet

The best analogy for how the Internet works is to compare it to the postal system. One way to communicate with someone living on the other side of the world is to send a letter. A postal carrier picks up the letter from the mailbox and delivers it to the post office. From there it travels to the post office near its final destination. Another postal carrier picks it up and delivers it to the recipient's address.

Internet Vocabulary Builder

domain name system (DNS) – a system that defines individual Internet hosts

domain – a system of organizing the Internet according to country or type of organization

When people use the Internet to send information, it is broken up into tiny packages called *packets*. These packets are routed through machines, aptly called *routers*, until they reach an address that is called a *server*. The server is equivalent to the local post office. The address on the information packets is an Internet Protocol (IP) address, for example 162.157.25.201. A server's IP address distinguishes it from all other computers on the Internet.

How does each packet of information find its way through a complex maze of computer networks stretching around the globe? Again, the analogy of the post office can be used. In a real-world post office, sorters read the address of the letter then sort it into the mailbag that is delivered to the destination post office. On the Internet, the packets are handled by routers that read the address. The packets are sent on the next part of the journey, until they arrive at the server and are reassembled. Users pick up their information by accessing the server.

The Anatomy of a Web Address

Teach students how to decipher a Web site address. Each time users log on to a Web site, they must type in a Web address. The Web address is actually the IP address of the server that stores the Web pages. If the IP address is 162.157.25.201, typing a series of numbers may be difficult to remember. To simplify the process, those numbers are translated into a special Web address called a Uniform Resource Locator (URL). Examine the diagram of a fictitious site on page 88.

Student Internet Activity: Top Domain Names

Overview

This activity will help students become familiar with the meanings of the top domain names in Web adresses. Use the diagram "The Anatomy of a Web Address" in conjunction with this activity.

What to Do

- In this activity, students will think about the top domain names for some Web addresses. Discuss the elements of a Web address. Photocopy the diagram "The Anatomy of a Web Address" and distribute to students.
- When students are comfortable with the format of an address, distribute copies of the "Top Domain Name" worksheet, page 89.
- Students can work independently or in pairs.
- During the activity, the following clues can be made available to those students who may require them:

    .com = a commercial business
    .edu = an educational institution
    .gov = a government organization
    .mil = a military organization
    .net = a network organization
    .org = a non-profit organization

- When students have completed the worksheet, follow up with a discussion of the abbreviations, what they mean, and why they are used.

The Anatomy of a Web Address

A Web address is written as a single, unbroken line with no spaces. Each part of the address identifies something. Examine this fictitious children's site as an example.

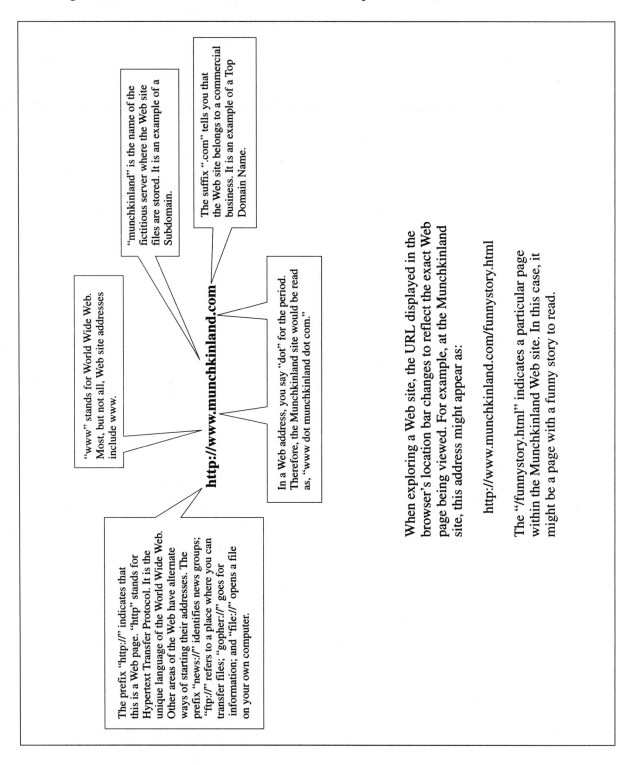

http://www.munchkinland.com

"www" stands for World Wide Web. Most, but not all, Web site addresses include www.

"munchkinland" is the name of the fictitious server where the Web site files are stored. It is an example of a Subdomain.

The suffix ".com" tells you that the Web site belongs to a commercial business. It is an example of a Top Domain Name.

In a Web address, you say "dot" for the period. Therefore, the Munchkinland site would be read as, "www dot munchkinland dot com."

The prefix "http://" indicates that this is a Web page. "http" stands for Hypertext Transfer Protocol. It is the unique language of the World Wide Web. Other areas of the Web have alternate ways of starting their addresses. The prefix "news://" identifies news groups; "ftp://" refers to a place where you can transfer files; "gopher://" goes for information; and "file://" opens a file on your own computer.

When exploring a Web site, the URL displayed in the browser's location bar changes to reflect the exact Web page being viewed. For example, at the Munchkinland site, this address might appear as:

http://www.munchkinland.com/funnystory.html

The "/funnystory.html" indicates a particular page within the Munchkinland Web site. In this case, it might be a page with a funny story to read.

Computer Activities for the Cooperative Classroom by Linda M. Schwartz and Kathlene R. Willing

Top Domain Name

Student Name _____

In North America, most Web addresses end with a dot and three letters.

1. Match the Domain Names with the correct group.

Top Domain Name	Sample Group
.com	an army base
.edu	a girl guide group
.gov	a clothing store
.mil	an elementary school
.net	a government tax office
.org	a worldwide Internet group

2. Match the appropriate Domain Name with these fictitious Web addresses.

Top Domain Name	Sample Group
.com	http://postoffice___
.edu	http://cookiesforsale___
.gov	http://artistweb___
.mil	http://fraserelementary___
.net	http://redcross___
.org	http://fortknox___

3. How do you think the Domain Names got their three-letter abbreviations?

_____

_____

_____

Computer Activities for the Cooperative Classroom by Linda M. Schwartz and Kathlene R. Willing

Top Domain Name	Sample Group
.com	– a clothing store
.edu	– an elementary school
.gov	– a state tax office
.mil	– an army base
.net	– a worldwide Internet group
.org	– a girl guide group

Top Domain Name	Sample Group
.com	http://postoffice.gov
.edu	http://cookiesforsale.com
.gov	http://artistweb.net
.mil	http://fraserelementary.edu
.net	http://redcross.org
.org	http://fortknox.mil

More Ideas

Challenge students to create their own fictitious Web addresses. Students work in pairs to create six domain names — one for each category. They exchange their Web addresses with a second pair of students for checking. When checking is complete, both pairs work together to categorize the addresses on six charts placed around the room. When all group work is finished, one representative from each group explains to the class where they placed their addresses and why.

Go Surf!

Use the URL below. Ask students to list ten domain extensions (.ca, .ru, .de). Challenge them to guess which country matches each domain. A world map may provide clues. When finished, students exchange and check answers.
http://www.domainit.com/country-domains.htm
Country Domains: A list of domain names from countries around the world.

Section 2   Make Friends With Your Browser

What Is a Browser?

Internet Vocabulary Builder

mosaic – the first graphical Web browser. It was created in the early 1990s, at the National Center for Supercomputing Applications.

A Web browser is like a friend. It follows the user when surfing the Net; remembers what the user likes on the Web; directs the user to sources of information; and allows the user to communicate with others.

A Web browser is specialized software. Most people tend to use either *Microsoft®*'s *Internet Explorer* browser or *Netscape Navigator* browser. However, there are many other browsers available. Today's Web browsers are designed with various special features. When launching a Web browser, the *Home page* of either *Microsoft®* or *Netscape* appears first. That is because the Home page has been set to go directly to that page each time the browser is launched.

Student Internet Activity: Make Friends With Your Browser

Overview

In "Make Friends With Your Browser" students get their "surfing legs" by acquainting themselves with the basic functions of a Web browser. Direct them to locate each of the functions noted on the "Make Friends With Your Browser" worksheet, page 92. The descriptions of the functions are:

- *Toolbar:* Is the row of buttons at the top of the browser. The buttons on the toolbar allow the user to navigate the Web.
- *Back:* Goes to the preceding Web page visited in that session.
- *Forward:* After using the Back button, the Forward button returns the user to the page just visited.
- *Stop:* Stops the browser from loading the current Web page. Click this button when a page is taking too long to load, or if a change of mind has occurred.
- *Reload or Refresh:* Reloads the current Web page. Use this if the page suddenly stops loading. Reload is also used to load the latest version of a Web page.
- *Home:* Goes to whatever page is the Home page — the first page that loaded when the browser was started.
- *Search:* Connects to Internet search engine pages.
- *Favorites or Bookmarks:* Is the place to save preferred Web sites.
- *Print*: Prints the Web page that appears in the browser window.
- *Location Bar:* The place in which the Web address is typed. The box may be called "Address," "Location," or "Go To" — depending on which browser is used.
- *Status Bar*: Is a narrow window at the bottom of the browser. It shows when a site has been contacted, and how much of the page has been downloaded. Watch this window when downloading a Web page.

What to Do

- Distribute the "Make Friends With Your Browser" worksheet, page 92, or simply verbalize the steps for a large group activity.

Answers to "Make Friends With Your Browser"

- Discuss the answers with the students, using the definitions/purposes noted in the activity Overview above.

Go Surf!

http://home.cnet.com/internet/0-3773.html
This site will tell you everything you need to know about Web browsers. Download the latest browser versions from *Microsoft®* or *Netscape*, for Windows and Mac. Try out one of the less well-known Web browsers. Ask students to check the tips and tutorials (included with most browsers) as well.

Tip: When a Web page is downloaded, it is temporarily stored on the user's computer. When going Back to that same page, the browser fetches that version of the page. If it is a page that changes frequently, like a news site, Reload gets the latest page.

Tip: *If you are using **Netscape Navigator**:* Go to the Edit Menu and select Preferences. On the Home page screen, type in the desired URL that will start each Web session. Not able to remember the address? Go to the Web site and copy the address that appears in the browser's Location Bar.

Tip: *If you are using **Internet Explorer**:* Depending on which version is being used, the Home page option will be found either under View and Options, or Tools and Internet Options. Type in the desired Web address, or simply select Use Current, if already on the Web page that is to be designated as Home.

Make Friends With Your Browser

Student Name _____

Find the following Buttons on the *Toolbar*. Describe what they do.

1. Toolbar:_____

   _____

2. Back: _____

   _____

3. Forward: _____

   _____

4. Stop: _____

   _____

5. Reload/Refresh: _____

   _____

6. Home: _____

   _____

7. Search: _____

   _____

8. Favorites/Bookmarks:_____

   _____

9. Print: _____

   _____

10. Location Bar: _____

    _____

11. Status Bar:_____

    _____

Computer Activities for the Cooperative Classroom by Linda M. Schwartz and Kathlene R. Willing

Section 3   You Be the Judge

Use the Internet Carefully

Use the Web to find information quickly. Search for a newspaper article, a speech by a famous person, or an idea for the school science fair. However, critical analysis is essential in evaluating information. Just because a Web site exists, does not mean that the information or pictures on the site are accurate — or even real!

Everything on the Web is not created equal! Initially students may be inclined to believe that everything they find on a Web site is true or reliable. Therefore, they need to be taught how to judge a site, before they gobble up its information. Students require guidance in developing the necessary skills to judge Web content. The following activity "You Be the Judge" provides a basic guideline that students can use.

Student Internet Activity: You Be the Judge

Overview

In "You Be the Judge" students ask themselves these basic questions when they visit any Web site:

- Who created the site?
- Why does the site exist?
- Is the information in the site up-to-date?
- Are the links relevant?
- Where did the information come from?

Working in pairs or small groups, students use a list of Web sites, chosen and previewed by the teacher. The Web sites should represent various formats, such as opinion sites, news sites, shopping sites, association sites, and government sites. Two evaluation worksheets are included for assessing Web sites.

What to Do

- Discuss the reason and value of the activity with the students.
- There are two worksheets for this activity. "You Be the Judge" is a question and answer sheet for in-depth analysis. "You Be the Judge Checklist" simply requires checking off "Yes" or "No" in response to the questions. Use either or both.
- Depending on the grade level, modify the number of Web sites to be evaluated. Since each site requires its own checklist, younger students may evaluate only one Web site at a given time. Expect older students to examine multiple sites. If all students evaluate the same site, make comparisons.
- Distribute the list of Web sites for students to evaluate. Provide each group with either a "You Be the Judge" worksheet (page 94) or checklist (page 95).

You Be the Judge

Student Name(s)_____

URL: _____

- When you visit a Web site, some of the information and graphics may seem interesting. However, just because they are on a Web site, does not mean the information is all true — or even real!

- Answer the following questions when you search through a Web site to find out if the information is reliable.

1. **Who created this site?**
   Scroll to the bottom of the page. Look for a copyright notice. It should explain who is responsible for the site — a person, a company, the government, or a school. It may have a link called "About this site" or "About us."

2. **Why does this site exist?**
   Is it trying to teach something, or convince you of something? Is it trying to persuade you to buy something? Does it ask for personal information, like your name or e-mail address?

3. **Is the information in this site up-to-date?**
   When was the site last updated? Is there a line that gives this information?

4. **Are the links relevant?**
   Where do the links go? Do all the linked sites have a similar point of view? Is there a strong bias?

5. **Where did the information come from?**
   Is the information someone's personal opinion or is it factual? Reliable sites include a list of resources, such as books or articles. Knowing where the content came from is important. Does the person or group behind the site believe very strongly in something?

Computer Activities for the Cooperative Classroom by Linda M. Schwartz and Kathlene R. Willing

You Be the Judge Checklist

Student Name(s)_____

URL: _____

- When you visit a Web site, some of the information and graphics may seem interesting. However, just because they are on a Web site, does not mean the information is all true — or even real!

- Use this checklist as you search and read information in a Web site. Answer the questions by putting a checkmark in the appropriate column.

How to Judge a Web Site	Yes	No
Does the site clearly state which group or individual created it?		
Does the site describe the group or individual's expertise?		
Is it trying to teach something, or convince you of something?		
Is the information up-to-date?		
Is there a date indicating when the site was created?		
Is there a date indicating when the site was last updated?		
Is there a phone number to get further information?		
Is there a mailing address to get further information?		
Is there an e-mail address to get further information?		
Are arguments or opinions clearly supported with facts?		
Can the information be verified on other Web sites, in books or magazines?		
Is it trying to persuade you to buy something?		
Is the information free of bias or stereotyping?		
Are there links to other useful sites?		
Do all the linked sites have a similar point of view?		
Is advertising kept separate from information?		
Does it ask for personal information, like your name or e-mail address?		

Computer Activities for the Cooperative Classroom by Linda M. Schwartz and Kathlene R. Willing

Go Surf!

http://forms.flashbase.com/forms/web_page_eval
Have students use this Web page to evaluate a Web site. They can submit the information and then view other sites that people have judged. Do they agree or disagree with the other evaluations?

Section 4   Finding What You Want

Is It Out There?

A textbook has an index to help find information. The Internet has many indexes called search engines. With the help of search engines, almost anything can be found on the Web. How do search engines work? They use automated *bots* or *spiders* that crawl around the Web 24 hours a day, examining Web pages. They retrieve information from Web pages, bring it back, and add it to the search engine's database.

Each search engine retrieves different pieces of information, such as the title of the page and the first twenty words on the page. Since each search engine has a unique database, and entering similar keywords produces different results, it is a good idea to Bookmark the following widely-used search engines for easy access to excellent search tools.

Alta Vista	www.altavista.com
Google	www.google.com
Excite	www.excite.com
Webcrawler	www.webcrawler.com
Lycos	www.lycos.com
Northern Light	www.northernlight.com
Yahoo	www.yahoo.com
Yahooligans	www.yahooligans.com

Internet Vocabulary Builder

search engine – an index that helps to find information on the Web.

spiders and bots (short for robots) – powerful indexing software that creates listings based on keywords.

Seek and you shall find. Maybe! Different search engines have different databases. This is why searching with the same key words using different search engines sometimes identifies different sources for the user.

Search Engine Tips
• Single word searches are too broad. Narrow the search by using two or three words. For example, instead of *dogs* try *poodle care*.
• Searching for a phrase produces results for multiple words. For example, *famous artists* retrieves pages on both *famous* and *artists*. For more precise searches, use quotation marks around the words. For example, *"famous artist"* searches for pages where those words appear side-by-side.
• Use Boolean operators (and, or, not) to narrow the search. For example, *vacation not beach* returns pages with the word *vacation*, but not the word *beach*.
• Another Boolean operator is the asterisk " * ". This is called *wildcard* searching. Use wildcards when unsure of the keyword's spelling. Also use them when looking for root words with different endings. For example, typing in *ski** returns sites that include the words "skier," "skis," and "skiing."

Student Internet Activity: Search Engine Challenge

Overview

Invite your students to be search engine "sleuths," by presenting them with a challenging research task. When they are done, they will be proud of the results of their search.

"Search Engine Challenge" asks students to find the ultimate chocolate chip cookie recipe. By conducting this Internet research, the students will test how a search engine responds to different key words within the same topic and to compare how different search engines respond to the same key words. By comparing and contrasting, students gain insights into the capabilities of various search engines.

Working in pairs, the students log on to the Internet, launch their Web browser, and surf to a designated search engine. Using key words from the "Search Engine Challenge" worksheet, they type in the key words to analyze the number of pages and hits, and record their observations.

Taste Test the Chocolate Chip Cookies! When "Search Engine Challenge" is completed, the "sleuths" print out the chocolate chip cookie recipes and take them home. Delectable treats can be shared with the class the next day!

What to Do

- Provide pairs of students with a copy of "Search Engine Challenge" worksheet, page 98. Students will find it helpful if you share the information from the Search Engine Tips on page 96. When the task is completed, students share the results with the class. Use the following questions to guide the discussion.
  - Which search strategy worked best? Why did it work best?
  - Which search strategy was least helpful? Why was it least helpful?
  - What was surprising about the results from a particular search engine?
  - How did different search engines compare? Were the sites similar or different?

Go Surf!

http://www.aj.com
- Have students make a list of questions. Go to the Ask Jeeves Web site to ask questions and get answers.

http://www.ajkids.com
- This site is specifically designed for children. Again, students can prepare questions and go to the Web site for answers.

Section 5   Communicating With Others

What Is An e-mail Address?

No stamp, no envelope, no mailbox! The Internet has revolutionized the way people communicate. A handwritten letter may take weeks to reach its final destination. An electronic message (e-mail) can be sent to a far-off recipient in seconds. Electronic mail is the most popular Internet application. In an e-mail address, the company that provides e-mail service has a domain name, such as *someplace.com*. The company is the *service provider*.

Internet Vocabulary Builder

spam – a mass electronic mailing that is unsolicited and indiscriminate; electronic junk mail. The term Spam may have originated in a Monty Python song, or in the computer lab at the University of Southern California, in reference to Spam lunchmeat.

Search Engine Challenge

Student Name(s)_____

Name of Search Engine _____

- Use this chart to record your observations.

- How many Web pages turned up for each search? Which search produced a chocolate chip cookie recipe on the first page of *hits* (results)? Record your observations.

Keyword(s) and Number of Pages	Number of Hits	Observations
recipes # of pages ___		
cookies # of pages ___		
cookies and recipes # of pages ___		
cookies not recipes # of pages ___		
"chocolate chip cookies" # of pages ___		

Computer Activities for the Cooperative Classroom by Linda M. Schwartz and Kathlene R. Willing

People who use electronic mail must have an e-mail address. It is like having a mailbox on the Internet. A typical e-mail address looks like this:

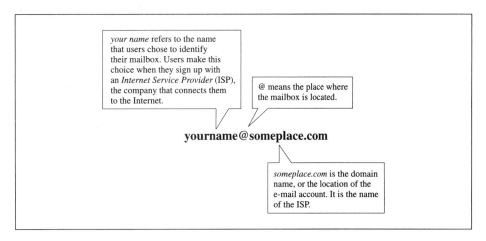

An e-mail program is used to send and receive e-mail messages. Popular applications include *Eudora®* and *Microsoft® Outlook*. Most Web browsers have their own built-in e-mail programs. E-mail can be sent without leaving the browser. Messages that are received may be kept in an *Inbox*. Copies of messages sent may be kept in the *Outbox*. Messages may be viewed, printed, and deleted using the buttons located in the application's Toolbar.

Student Internet Activity: Communicating With Others

Overview

In "Communicating With Others," students open their e-mail program and locate each part of an e-mail message as the teacher describes it.

After students have been introduced to the main parts of an e-mail message, they can practice sending messages to each other. "Communicating With Others" can be integrated into the curriculum by:

- exchanging e-mail messages as the characters in a novel study or a play (Romeo sends an e-mail to Juliet);
- creating an electronic *continuous story* that is added to each time an e-mail message is opened;
- designating student math experts and inviting other students to query them by e-mail; and
- using the school *intranet* (internal network) to collaborate with another class that is studying a similar unit.

What to Do

- Start "Communicating with Others" by providing students with a copy of the "Student e-mail Etiquette," on page 101. Review it together, then walk them through their e-mail program.

Go Surf!

http://www.netramp.net/about-email-addresses.htm
Students can explore this site for background information on e-mail.

Tip: If there is no e-mail program installed on the school's computers, then log on to www.yahoo.com. Click on *e-mail* at the top of the screen, and have students set up fictitious accounts. Be cautious and emphatic! Instruct students not to include any personal or factual information.

The Anatomy of an e-mail Message

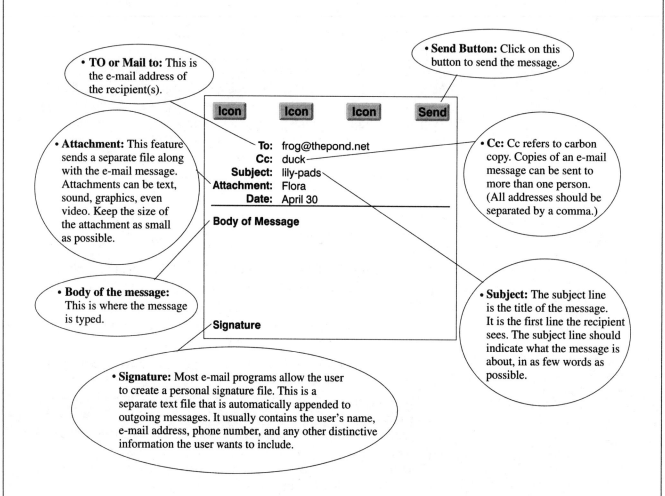

• **TO or Mail to:** This is the e-mail address of the recipient(s).

• **Send Button:** Click on this button to send the message.

• **Attachment:** This feature sends a separate file along with the e-mail message. Attachments can be text, sound, graphics, even video. Keep the size of the attachment as small as possible.

• **Cc:** Cc refers to carbon copy. Copies of an e-mail message can be sent to more than one person. (All addresses should be separated by a comma.)

To: frog@thepond.net
Cc: duck
Subject: lily-pads
Attachment: Flora
Date: April 30

Body of Message

Signature

• **Body of the message:** This is where the message is typed.

• **Subject:** The subject line is the title of the message. It is the first line the recipient sees. The subject line should indicate what the message is about, in as few words as possible.

• **Signature:** Most e-mail programs allow the user to create a personal signature file. This is a separate text file that is automatically appended to outgoing messages. It usually contains the user's name, e-mail address, phone number, and any other distinctive information the user wants to include.

Computer Activities for the Cooperative Classroom by Linda M. Schwartz and Kathlene R. Willing

Student e-mail Etiquette

Student Name _____

_____ Give people a hint about what is in your e-mail message. Write a brief, descriptive subject line. That way, people who receive a lot of e-mail know quickly why you are writing to them.

_____ Be very careful about what you say in your message. E-mail can be easily stored, sent on to other people, or printed. You never know who will see what you write.

_____ Try to keep your e-mail message brief and to the point. The more words in your message, the more time it takes to download and read it.

_____ DON'T USE CAPITAL LETTERS. Capitals make it appear that you are SHOUTING. Capitals also make it difficult to read your message.

_____ Check your message carefully for grammar, spelling, and punctuation. Remember, e-mail is just another form of communication, and you want to make a good impression.

_____ Never pretend that you are someone else when you send e-mail messages. It is unfair and could lead to a lawsuit.

_____ Never post another person's e-mail message to a Web site or online discussion group without permission. This is disrespectful, and it could be illegal.

Computer Activities for the Cooperative Classroom by Linda M. Schwartz and Kathlene R. Willing

Section 6   Respecting the Work of Others

Sharing Ideas on the Internet

Since the Internet is about sharing, it is a good source for shareware. Everything from classroom management tools, to math games and science lessons can be downloaded. However, shareware users sometimes neglect to register or pay for these programs should they decide to use them. Such misuse results in developers not being compensated or acknowledged for their work.

Internet Etiquette

Ask students what they think it means to be a responsible Internet citizen. Because the Internet is a diverse community of millions of users with no formal policing in place, it is necessary to observe online protocol. This "code of conduct" is called "Netiquette." Follow the rules of Netiquette for smooth online sailing. Ignore those rules, and you risk offending others and being "flamed" — having rude messages sent to you by angry users.

Student Internet Activity: How to Cite Internet Resources

Overview

Information is quickly shared and exchanged on the Internet. This instant and effortless access can make plagiarism very tempting. It is too easy for students to copy the work of others on the Internet and claim it as their own. Therefore, it is imperative that they be taught how to properly cite references. Just as there are correct ways for students to cite books and magazines, there are correct ways to cite online resources for inclusion in a bibliography. This activity shows students how.

What to Do

- Provide students with a copy of the "How to Cite Internet Resources," page 103, which they can keep in their reference folders. Post an enlarged copy of the page in the computer area.

Student Internet Activity: Respecting the Work of Others

Overview

"Respecting the Work of Others" creates a forum for students to discuss ethical computer use. The organization, *Computer Ethics Institute,* has developed *"The Ten Commandments of Computer Ethics."* These commandments will help guide students in applying ethical practices to their computing. Working at the computer in small groups, students use the Internet to access the Computer Ethics Institute Web site, where they select one commandment and discuss its meaning.

What to Do

- Organize the students into small groups and have them access the Web. Provide students with chart paper to record their findings and the URL of the Computer Ethics Institute.
  http://www.brook.edu/its/cei/cei_hp.htm

Internet Vocabulary Builder

shareware – software made available on the honor system for a nominal fee. Upon payment, the user is registered with the developer and receives support and updates.

Copycats Beware! Since the problem of copying is so pervasive, Web sites exist for the purpose of scanning students' papers for possible copyright infringement. Specially designed search tools crawl the Web to find a match of similar phrases to the student's work. When a match appears, the teacher is alerted.

How to Cite Internet Resources

Electronic Mail

Structure: Author of e-mail message. Subject line of the message. [Online] Available e-mail: student@address.edu from author@address.edu. Date of message.

Example: Smith, Steven. Rainfall statistics question. [Online] Available e-mail: student1@redschoolhouse.edu from steve@meterologycentre.gov. March 15, 2000.

Worldwide Web

Structure: Author. Title of item. [Online] Available http://address/filename, date of document or download.

Example: Lawson, Margaret. How to cite Internet resources. [Online] Available http://www.somewhere.net/resources.html, May 5, 2000.

Usenet Newsgroups

Structure: Author. Title of item. [Online] Available usenet: group, date of post.

Example: Sola, Meline. Learning to use the Internet. [Online] Available usenet: k12.ed.research, June 2, 2000.

Online Images

Structure: Description or title of image. [Online image] Available http://address/filename Web, date of download.

Example: Cub climbing a tree. [Online image] Available http://sdzoo.net/pub/cub/GIF, September 15, 2000.

- Instruct students to create a two-column chart with the commandment as the title, so they can record their discussion. In column one, students list "Why the commandment is important." In column two, they predict the "Consequences of not observing it." When the charts are complete, each group presents their findings to the class. (Younger students can complete this activity orally, without recording their discussion.)

Go Surf!

- Students can go to the MLA Citation Guide for further information on citing resources.
  http://www.bedfordstmartins.com/online/citex.html

Section 7   WebQuests

Internet Vocabulary Builder

WebQuest – a collaborative model for classroom Internet projects, integrating inquiry-based learning with use of the Web

Integrating the Web and Curriculum

In 1995, Bernie Dodge, a professor of educational technology at San Diego State University, developed a model for integrating the use of the Web, to teach any subject at any grade level. He called his work a WebQuest, and posted a summary of his idea on the Web. Since then educators around the world have incorporated WebQuests into their curricula.

In a WebQuest, students are sent on a quest for knowledge. They are directed to online resources within the context of a specific curriculum mission. Rather than accessing textbooks which may be dated, or filtered CD-ROM encyclopedias, WebQuests expose students to a wide range of online sources, such as subject experts, directories of information, databases, current news, and all manner of interest groups. They must critically evaluate and extract relevant information in order to construct meaning within the context of the goal. WebQuests may be conducted independently or in small groups. Since cooperation is essential in a group setting, students gain experience in teamwork.

WebQuests teach a process that can be applied to all curricular areas. Students become confident Web explorers and begin to make connections between the WebQuest process and broader Web exploration.

The Elements of a WebQuest

A well-designed WebQuest incorporates the following components:

- **Introductory information** – sets the stage for the WebQuest and stimulates student curiosity. It may be presented as a role playing activity.
- **Main task** – describes the ultimate goal of the WebQuest. This may take the form of a presentation or a written assignment.
- **Resources** – provides a list of appropriate grade-level resources, including Web pages that have been previewed by the teacher, as well as traditional offline materials. They help students complete the WebQuest. Students do not necessarily need to access all of the resources listed. Advise your students accordingly.
- **Process** – acts as a step-by-step guide for completing the WebQuest. Process includes hints or tips to complete the task, such as printing instructions, brainstorming with team members, or creating presentation materials.

- **Advice** – provides practical hints on how to organize information. Present it as a checklist or as a list of questions. It may also be given as instructions to complete timelines, maps, or posters.
- **Evaluation** – informs students how they will be evaluated. Teachers may wish to create a rubric collaboratively with students, following the suggestions in Chapter 2.
- **Conclusion** – brings closure to the WebQuest and encourages students to extend the experience into other areas of the curriculum. Many WebQuests conclude by having students post their findings on a student-created Web site.

For an initial WebQuest experience, it is easier to have students complete a ready-made WebQuest online. These can be found on Web sites, such as The Teachers First WebQuest Collection (see "Go Surf," below). When teachers have become familiar and comfortable with the WebQuest technique, they can design a unique WebQuest relevant to their curriculum needs.

Student Internet Activity: Rainforest WebQuest

Overview

"Rainforest WebQuest" is a quest for knowledge. Students work in groups of three to role play travel consultants. They do research on Australia on behalf of a construction company planning to build a resort near a rainforest. To complete this task, the consultants use the resources supplied in the WebQuest and go in search of the required information. When the groups have completed their quests, they make a presentation to the construction company (the class).

What to Do

- An Internet connection is essential for doing a WebQuest.
- This activity includes Internet links. The activity is provided as a sample to copy (scan/type) into a word processing application. Save the document and then make it available to students.
- When the students are connected to the Internet, they can complete the WebQuest on computer. If they are using an application that does not support "hot links," instruct students to copy and paste the URL into the location bar of the browser.
- Introduce the WebQuest and direct students to where the WebQuest instructions have been saved.

Go Surf!

- This site is a collection of WebQuests.
  http://www.teachersfirst.com/WebQuest.htm
  The Teachers First WebQuest Collection

- Matrix of Example WebQuests. This site is a list of Web sites that was developed by student teachers, experienced teachers, library/media specialists, and others.
  http://edweb.sdsu.edu/webquest/matrix.html

- Building Blocks of a WebQuest. This site provides information on structuring a WebQuest.
  http://edweb.sdsu.edu/people/bdodge/webquest/buildingblocks.html

No Site in Sight? Sites can become obsolete over time. Although specific Web sites are recommended, it is not uncommon for sites to change, or even disappear. Use search engines and the specific key words to find current sites that will replace those that are no longer accessible.

Hot Link Tip: Some applications, such as *Microsoft® Word*, automatically convert URLs into "hot links," which makes it possible to connect directly to the Internet. Other applications may support starting the browser from the word processing document. Consult the online Help Index and search for "links" or "hot links."

Rainforest WebQuest

Description

- You are a travel consultant. A construction company has sent you to look into building a resort near an Australian rainforest. You have arrived and you are ready to start exploring.

Task

- You must report to your boss (the teacher) about the rainforest, the vegetation, the animals, and the people who live nearby. Include a picture of the rainforest and reasons why people may want to stay at a resort near a rainforest.

Resources

Use the following resources for your research.

- This site describes the animals that live in an Australian rainforest.
  http://www.smithfieshs.qld.edu.au/wet_tropics/animals.html
- This site describes the aborigines living in the rainforest.
  http://rainforest-australia.com/aborigin.htm
- This site is a great place to start your search for anything and everything about Australian rainforests.
  http://rainforest-australia.com/Site%20Map.htm

Process

- Visit each of the three Web sites listed above. Assign one person in your group to research animals, one to research vegetation, and one to research people. Open a word processing document and multi-task to take notes on the information you find.
- Your group will do a presentation. As a group, cooperatively decide on: what to include in the presentation; the responsibilities of each member; and how to present (*Power Point*®, *HyperStudio*®, poster boards, lecture format…). Each person participates in the presentation. Pictures and diagrams are expected.

Advice

- Narrow your search to three or four interesting topics. List five to ten facts about each topic. Add this list to your word processing document.

Evaluation

- Evaluation will be based on your notes, presentation, participation and teamwork, and final conclusion. The criteria are to:
  - identify and describe the animals and plants;
  - describe the society;
  - formulate questions that assess advantages and disadvantages of the project;
  - describe the impact of the project on the food supply and the society; and
  - use appropriate vocabulary.

Conclusion

- List three things you learned about gathering information on the Internet. Add them to your word processing document. Use these skills whenever you use the Internet for a project.

Computer Activities for the Cooperative Classroom by Linda M. Schwartz and Kathlene R. Willing

Professional Resources

Baker, E. 1997. "Model-Based Performance Assessment." *Theory into Practice.* v. 36 n. 4, pp. 247–54.

Bateman, J., et. al. 1991. *Touching Tomorrow Today: Integrating the Computer into the Elementary School.* North York, ON: North York Board of Education.

Bennet, B., Rolheiser, C., and Stevhan, S. 1991. *Cooperative Learning: Where Heart Meets Mind.* Toronto, ON: Educational Connections.

Benson, B. and Barnett, S. 1999. *Student-Led Conferencing Using Showcase Portfolios.* Thousand Oaks, CA: Corwin Press, Inc.

Burness, P. Exec. Ed. 1997. *Learn & Live.* Nicasio, CA: George Lucas Foundation.

Classroom Connect: The K–12 Educator's Guide to the Internet. El Segundo, CA: Classrooom Connect, Inc.

Conderman, G., Hatcher, R.E., and Ikan, P.A. Sum 1998. "Why Student-Led Conferencing Works." *Kappa Delta Pi Record.* v. 34 n. 4, pp. 132–34.

Day, V., Skidmore, M. 1996. "Linking Performance Assessment and Curriculum Goals." *Teaching Exceptional Children.* v. 29 n. 1, pp. 59–64.

Eddings, J. 1994. *How the Internet Works.* Emeryville, CA: Ziff-Davis Press.

Gronlund, N.E. 1970. *Stating Behavioral Objectives for Classroom Instruction.* New York, NY: MacMillan Company.

Herman, L.P. and Morrell, M. Jun 1999. "Educational Progressions: Electronic Portfolios in a Virtual Classroom." *T.H.E. Journal.* v. 26 n. 11, pp. 86–88.

Johnson, D.W. 1999. *Learning Together and Alone: Cooperative, Competitive, and Individualistic Learning,* 5th ed. Boston, MA: Allyn and Bacon.

Johnson, D.W. and Johnson, R.T. Spr 1999, "Making Cooperative Learning Work." *Theory into Practice.* v. 38 n. 2, pp. 67–73.

Johnson, D.W., Johnson, R.T. and Holubec, E.J. 1990. *Cooperation in the Classroom* (rev. ed.). Edina, MN: Interaction Book Company.

Heide, A., Stilborne, L. 1996. *The Teacher's Complete and Easy Guide to the Internet,* 2nd ed. Toronto, ON: Trifolium Books, Inc.

Klein, A. Jan.–Feb. 1996. "6 Ways to Assess Writing." *Instructor.* v. 105 n. 5, p. 44.

Koch, R. and Schwartz-Petterson, J. 2000. *The Portfolio Guidebook: Implementing Quality in an Age of Standards*. Norwood, MA: Christopher Gordon Publishers, Inc.

Paris, S. G. and Ayers, L.R. 1994. *Becoming Reflective Students and Teachers with Portfolios and Authentic Assessment*. Washington, DC: American Psychological Association.

Reinhardt, P. 1997. *Making Best Use of the INTERNET to Enhance Classroom Instruction (Grades 3–6): Resource Handbook*. Bellevue, WA: Bureau of Education and Research.

Rolheiser, C., Bower, B., and Stevhan, S. 2000. *The Portfolio Organizer: Succeeding with Portfolios in your Classroom.* Alexandria, VA: Association for Supervision and Curriculum Development.

Schipper, B. and Rossi, J. 1997. *Portfolios in the Classroom: Tools for Learning and Instruction*. Portland, ME: Stenhouse Publishers.

Smith, Frank. *Insult to Intelligence*. 1986. New York, NY: Arbor House.

Taggart, G.L., Phifer, S.J., Nixon, J.A., and Wood, M. 1998. *Rubrics: a Handbook for Construction and Use*. Technomic Publishing.

The Staff of Classroom Connect. 1997. *Internet Homework Helper*, Lancaster, PA, Wentworth Worldwide Media, Inc.

Willing, K.R. and Girard S. 1990. *Learning Together: computer integrated classrooms*. Toronto, ON: Pembroke Publishers Ltd.

Online Resources

- AskERIC, the Educational Resources Information Center
  http://ericir.syr.edu/

- Classroom Connect's lesson plan database
  http://www.classroom.net/home.asp

- Searchable database of integrated Internet activities from Link2learn
  http://l2lpd.arin.k12.pa.us/success/

- Cyberpilot's License, a comprehensive collection of resources on Web ethics
  http://www.cwrl.utexas.edu/~burniske/cpl/

- K–12 Resource Jump Page, links to search tools, lesson plans, educational listservs and more
  http://mustang.coled.umn.edu/Exploration/resource/Resource.html

- Intercultural Classroom Connections, a free service that links teachers with other classrooms in search of collaborative e-mail projects
  http://www.iecc.org/

- ThinkQuest, http://io.advanced.org/ThinkQuest/I-stylehtml, January 8, 1996

Appendix

Directory of Software and Software Publishers referred to in this book

Adobe Systems Incorporated
345 Park Avenue
San Jose, CA 95110-2704
800-833-6687
http://www.adobe.com

Adobe Illustrator®
Adobe Pagemaker®

Apple, Inc
1 Infinite Loop
Cupertino, CA 95014
800-692-7753
http://www.apple.com

AppleWorks®
HyperCard®
Quicktime™

Bytes of Learning
60 Renfrew Drive, Suite 210
Markham, ON L3R 0E1
800-465-6428
http://www.bytesoflearning.com

UltraKey™
MP Express™

e*media, inc.
405 B Little Lake Drive
Ann Arbor, MI 48103
734-669-4495
http://sarahspage.com/

Sarah's Page Web Builder©

FileMaker, Inc
5201 Patrick Henry Drive
Santa Clara, CA 95054
800-325-2747
http://www.filemaker.com

FileMaker® Pro

Ingenuity Works
1123 Fir Ave.
Blaine, WA 98230-9702
1-800-665-0667
http://www.ingenuityworks.com

All the Right Type™

Knowledge Adventure
19840 Pioneer Avenue
Torrance, CA 90503
800-545-7677
http://www.knowledgeadventure.com
http://hyperstudio.com

Typing Tutor
HyperStudio™

The Learning Company School Division
500 Redwood Blvd.
Novato, CA 94947
800-358-9144
http://www.learningcompany.com

Kid Pix Studio™ *Deluxe*
The Amazing Writing Machine®
Mavis Beacon Teaches Typing!®
Oregon Trail®

Macromedia®
600 Townsend Street
San Francisco, CA 94103
415-252-2000
http://macromedia.com

Macromedia® *Dreamweaver*™

Microsoft
One Microsoft Way
Redmond, WA 98052-6399
800-426-9400
http://www.microsoft.com

Microsoft® *Word*®
Microsoft® *Excel*®
Microsoft® *Works*®
Microsoft® *Power Point*®
Microsoft® *Front Page Editor*®
Microsoft® *Outlook*®

QUALCOMM Incorporated
5775 Morehouse Drive
San Diego, CA 92121
858-587-1122
http://www.qualcomm.com

Eudora®

Sunburst Technology
101 Castleton Street
Pleasantville, NY 10570
800-321-7511
http://www.sunburst.com

Type to Learn™
(Trademark of Houghton-Mifflin)
Web Workshop™ *PRO*

Tom Snyder Productions
80 Coolidge Hill Road
Watertown, MA 02472
800-321-7511
http://www.teachTSP.com

Community Construction Kit™
Neighborhood Map Machine™
Timeliner™
Mpower™

Typin's Cool™
Suite 401, 176 Gloucester Street
Ottawa, ON
K2P 0A6
800-267-2587
http://www.typins-cool.com

Typin's Cool™

Index